CARS THE OLD CLASSICS

OXR 215

CARS THE OLD CLASSICS

FROM THE EARLY DAYS TO 1945

Andrew Whyte

Author's note

I have tried to give *Cars: The Old Classics* a geographical pattern, to aid the reader's route through motoring history. That history has taken place almost entirely in the European and North American continents, with France claiming the majority of 'firsts'. I have therefore chosen to 'travel' around Europe anti-clockwise, starting in France and ending in Britain, before crossing the Atlantic to conclude each chapter in the USA. Only at the beginning of the first chapter, which deals with the 'pre-motor car' era, does the sequence vary.

The 'journey' begins in earnest at the turn of the century. Andrew Whyte

ENDPAPERS *A special coupé on the 1930 Bentley Speed Six chassis: superb coachwork by Gurney Nutting for Woolf Barnato, Bentley's chief financier.*

PAGE 1 *Hispano-Suiza, 1931, with Swiss and Spanish emblems on the radiator. The stork of Lorraine mascot was borne by Hispano-Suizas from 1918. It had been the symbol of Georges Guynemer's squadron of Hispano-Suiza-engined SPAD fighters in World War I.*

PAGES 2–3 *Rolls-Royce built the Phantom II from 1929 to 1935. Coachbuilders Thrupp & Maberly made this fixed-head coupé for Prince Aly Khan in 1932.*

THIS PAGE *Typical of British quality sports cars of the vintage era, the rakish Alvis 12/50 was introduced in 1923. This is the famous Duck's Back model of that year.*

Contents

First published in 1983 by Octopus Books Limited
59 Grosvenor Street, London W1

ISBN 0 86273 072 4
Reprinted 1984
Produced by Mandarin Publishers Limited
22a Westlands Road,
Quarry Bay, Hong Kong

Printed in Hong Kong

A CLASSIC ERA DAWNS

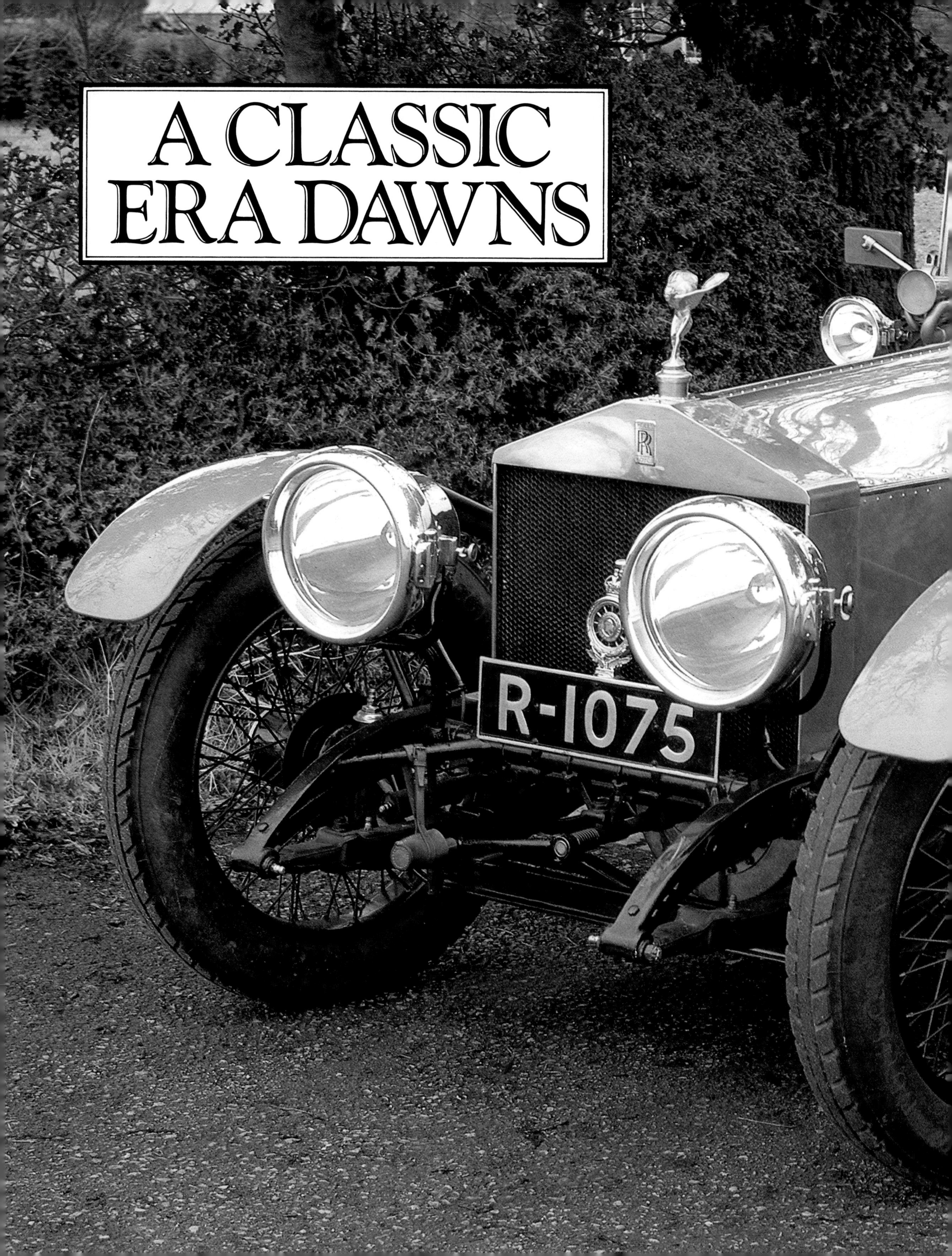

PRECEDING PAGES *The Rolls-Royce 40/50, dubbed 'Silver Ghost', established for the marque its reputation as the world's best car. This is the vehicle which completed the entire journey from London to Edinburgh in top gear (see page 18).*
ABOVE *The existing link: Cugnot's amazing tractor of 1771. It has a twin-cylinder single-action steam engine and is the oldest surviving self-propelled road vehicle in the world.*
RIGHT *Amédée Bollée of Le Mans was the most noteworthy maker of early steam carriages. This example, dating from 1873, is one of the earliest.*

The motor car has become an everyday item in people's lives, but it is nevertheless remarkable for the way it affects so many of them. In that sense the car is a classic invention. But what exactly is meant by 'classic'? Whether used or abused, it is a word with a wealth of meaning; but most people would agree that 'classic' means something generally accepted to be of the highest rank or class. And for achievement alone, the six decades from 1885 to 1945 must count as the classic period for motoring and the motor car.

Many centuries earlier, with the 'fire chariots' of the Chinese Chou dynasty, man had had the knowledge of steam power. It may have been reading about those 'chariots' that inspired the Flemish Jesuit and astronomer, Father Ferdinand Verbiest. He was part of the mission to China, and died there in 1688. He wrote a book in which he included his own design for a steam car; it had four wheels, plus a fifth wheel on a hinged arm to steer it. In the centre of the main bodywork was a coal-burning hearth with a retort, or flask-like container with an angled neck, mounted above it. Steam from the retort's nozzle was aimed at a disc with protruding steps around its rim, like a waterwheel. The high-pressure jet made this horizontally mounted disc rotate. Simple gearing took this rotation to one of the pairs of wheels on the ground.

The model, Verbiest claimed, would run for an hour or even longer, but the evidence in this case is merely the written word. The evidence of nearly a century later is much more tangible. It can be felt and touched and, with very special permission, sat upon by visitors to the Conservatoire Nationale des Arts et Métiers in Paris. This important landmark in motoring history is the Cugnot steam car.

Nicolas Joseph Cugnot, a French army officer, made his model in 1763 and, six years later, became the world's first motorist when he demonstrated his invention to his government sponsors. Although it could travel at only a slow walking pace, the Cugnot vehicle supposedly crashed. This first car has not survived. In 1771, however, Cugnot completed another vehicle—similar but larger, although it was never developed, probably because it was too sophisticated. Truly it was more of a gun-pulling tractor in design, but a change of management at the war office left Cugnot's backers in a minority.

Although it was never used, the Cugnot was stored away on military premises until 1800, by which time the more technological nations of the world were just beginning to see new uses for steam. In that year someone was wise enough to have the Cugnot steam machine placed in the Conservatoire.

The Cugnot *was* crude, with its huge wood-fired copper boiler suspended ahead of a single front wheel (turning when it turned), an overall length of 7.3 m (24 ft), width and height more than 2.1 m (7 ft), a pair of rear wheels over 1.8 m (6 ft) in diameter, and no springing of any kind. On the other hand, it had some brilliant innovations, such as a modern-style steering system, mechanical front-wheel drive, and an automatic steam pressure supply to the single action, two-cylinder power unit. Cugnot was the first motorist, but it would still be a long time before he was recognized as such.

In other countries, the power of steam was also appreciated. First for Britain was William Murdoch, a Scottish engineer who worked for a company specializing in steam pumps for Cornish tin mines. One of the firm's directors was James Watt, who had already worked on a road vehicle project but had abandoned it because of business priorities. In 1784, Murdoch's steam carriage, with cranked axle drive like a pedal car, made its legendary début, frightening everyone in the immediate vicinity. Another part of the legend is Watt's jealousy of Murdoch, who was then kept so busy that his carriage was never developed.

It was left to Robert Trevithick, in 1801, to build a road machine capable of carrying several people uphill under power. America was to follow European countries in becoming a great car-making nation; but it was a Welshman, Oliver Evans, who started the ball rolling there in 1787 by obtaining a patent for a steam-powered vehicle from the Maryland authorities. (Registering a new design or invention at a patent office ensures that it cannot be used by others without permission.)

Throughout the 19th century, inventors and speculators went their different ways, building steam carriages of all shapes and sizes. Most significant was the persistence shown by the Frenchman Amédée Bollée, a Le Mans bellfounder. He made a series of steam wagons, and his elder son continued the work. A fine example can be seen today in Compiègne's Musée National de la Voiture et du Tourisme.

In 1860 another Frenchman, Jean Joseph Etienne Lenoir, patented a simple gas engine and fitted it to a vehicle which ran in May 1862. Exploding a mixture of hydrogen and air in an enclosed space had been achieved earlier in the century, but Lenoir's effort was another 'first' for France. It was a Frenchman, too—Alphonse Beau de Rochas—who sketched the four-stroke principle in 1862, and this is the system still used in the modern car engine. The principle is based on four piston operations: the piston sucks in the fuel; compresses it; the fuel is ignited; and then the piston rises to release the exhaust gases.

For the achievement of a practical internal combustion engine, however, the turning point in the creation of the motor car, it is necessary to look at what was happening in

Germany, where Dr Nikolaus Otto—inspired by Beau de Rochas—constructed a reliable four-stroke gas engine in 1876. Four years earlier Otto, a partner in the Deutz engine company at Cologne, had been joined by two inventive young engineers, Gottlieb Daimler and Wilhelm Maybach. The relationship with Otto became rather bitter, however, and in 1882 Daimler left to start his own engine workshop at Bad Cannstatt near Stuttgart, taking Maybach with him. The outcome was the definitive Daimler liquid-fuelled, four-stroke engine for which the patent DRP 28002 was granted on 16 December 1883. This historic unit is considered the first petrol engine, where the fuel was ignited in the cylinders to drive the pistons.

Daimler saw his engines as 'attachments' rather than integral features of a vehicle, designing them for use in existing types of road and rail carriage and in boats. It was probably his disciple, Maybach, who persuaded Daimler that he should make a roadgoing vehicle of his own and the result was their hobbyhorse-style motorcycle of 1885.

In the same year, not far away, in Mannheim, the first real motor car was completed. Karl Benz, the man responsible, deserves his place in history, even though his car had only three wheels: it could just as easily have had four. His 1885 single-cylinder design, which he had planned as a complete vehicle, was granted the basic patent DRP 37435 on 29 January 1886. Within a year Benz's rivals Daimler and Maybach had a four-wheeled car on the road. The motor industry had begun.

The car takes shape

From then on, development was rapid, France stealing the thunder once again, as so often in motoring history.

Gottlieb Daimler, who had aged prematurely and was to die in 1900 at 65, had put his French patents in the hands of a Belgian friend, living in Paris, called Edouard Sarazin. Soon after Sarazin's death in 1886 his widow married Emile Levassor who, with his partner René Panhard, had been making carpentry equipment. They now acquired the Daimler patents and created the 'shape' of the orthodox car with their Système Panhard et Levassor: the idea was to have the engine at the front, coupled to a gearbox and driving through chains to the back axle.

LEFT *The first car: the 1.7-litre, single-cylinder Benz of 1885 had belt-and-chain drive, water-cooling and elliptic springs as shown. Today the layout would be termed 'mid-engined'.*

ABOVE *The Daimler-Maybach partnership produced the world's first motorcycle in 1885. Their first four-wheeler was this converted carriage, fitted in 1886 with Daimler's engine.*

There were three other French pioneers. The Peugeot family firm started in hardware manufacture. From 1885 the concern made bicycles, and in 1889 a steam car. The latter was built in conjunction with Léon Serpollet, whose flash boiler, which enabled steam to be raised quickly by the instantaneous evaporation of water in heated multiple tubes, caused him to be dubbed the 'Bugatti' of the steam car scene. Soon, however, the Peugeot concern was buying Daimler's internal combustion engines from Emile Levassor.

Among the most productive of the classic French pioneers were the Count de Dion and Georges Bouton. After ten years of steam vehicle manufacture, they began producing modern petrol engines for themselves and other vehicle makers; their greatest claim to fame is the de Dion principle of driving the rear wheels through universally jointed shafts, using a solid axle tube simply to carry the wheels. This system is still used today.

While we are still in 19th-century France, the Renault brothers—Louis, Marcel, and Fernand—must be mentioned. Working in a garden shed, the solemn, 21-year-old Louis Renault used a de Dion engine in his first voiturette (a French term for a light car) of 1898, by which time there can have been few large cities that did not boast a vehicle maker of some description.

Like the other manufacturers, the Renaults were highly competitive and became involved in motor racing – that exciting, commercial, often tragic sport which first took place on the dusty roads of France. Two of the pioneers already mentioned, Emile Levassor and Marcel Renault, lost their lives in racing accidents. Some say the first true race was the one in Paris organized by M. Fossier of the *Vélocipède* magazine as early as 1887, in which the only competing 'car' was Count de Dion's steam quadricycle. Certainly, the count was the first race winner by any interpretation, because his steam tractor beat a small horde of internal combustion-engined Peugeots and Panhards in the first-ever inter-city event, from Paris to Rouen in 1894. The count averaged 18.7 km/h (11.6 mph) for the distance, which was just under 130 km (80 miles). However, steam would not stay ahead for long.

All the activity in France tended to overshadow motoring development in other countries. The first all-Italian petrol-driven car was the Lanza of 1895; but Michele Lanza built only a few of these machines. It was FIAT, at the turn of the century, that was to put Italy 'into gear'. FIAT's chief founder, Giovanni Agnelli, had once suggested partnership to Lanza, but Lanza preferred to give priority to his original business of candle-making.

Austria also had its pioneers. First of all came the visionary Siegfried Marcus, who was undoubtedly one of the world's first car makers—but what he did seems quite unconnected with subsequent work in Central Europe. Much advanced engineering was to originate from the Austro-Hungarian region, and at this stage it should be noted that Ferdinand Porsche's illustrious career began there in the last century. In 1898, at the age of 23, he joined former coachbuilder Jacob Lohner who adopted Porsche's petrol-electric design. In this, a petrol engine was used to generate power for electric motors mounted in the road wheels, thus dispensing with normal transmission. Professor Porsche had an important place in motoring history. After his years with Auto Union and Volkswagen, he went on to establish his own company, now one of the most famous sports car manufacturers in the world.

Britain was not short of brilliant engineers, despite the fact that its classics-to-be were not part of the first wave of this newfangled automobilism. The British were, in general, as sceptical as any nation about the future of motoring. Many an argument was lost because trains ran on their special rails and therefore were acceptable, whereas the motor car could lurch hither and thither and make the roads unsafe for all. Early importers in the form of wealthy gentry must have helped the popular idea that motoring had no place in the British way of life and should be curbed. 'A new French sporting craze' was the favourite headline for brief reports on the 1894 Paris–Rouen race.

Few British cars existed then. Although the Butler motor tricycle was shown at an exhibition in 1885, steam engineer John Henry Knight's 1895 four-wheeler (converted from three) was probably the first British petrol-engined car to run. Neither reached production stage. Nevertheless Britain's true beginnings as a motoring nation date back to 1895, with the birth of the Lanchester and the Wolseley as prototypes. Two of the Lanchester brothers, Frederick and George, were brilliant designers—although in different ways and at different times. The third brother, Frank, had a flair for diplomacy and was destined to sell fleets of Lanchester cars to Indian royalty. In 1895, though, it was the originality of Frederick Lanchester's ideas—going back to first principles rather than using old systems based on carriages—that made his company Britain's first truly classic marque. In fact, *Autocar* magazine once stated that Lanchester was responsible for half the primary features of the modern car, especially in the areas of chassis stiffness, transmission and suspension. Also, the twin-cylinder power unit ran much more smoothly than other cars of the day.

Herbert Austin's first car was a three-wheeler, similar to the Léon Bolleé (designed by the younger son of that famous French family). At that time, Austin worked for the Wolseley Sheep Shearing Machine Company of Birmingham, after which his first designs were named.

In 1896, after much lobbying, the raising of the speed limit to 12 mph (19 km/h)—from 4 mph (6.5 km/h) in the country and 2 mph (3 km/h) in the towns—set Britain on its course to catch up with the inevitable march of progress on the Continent and in America. In that year, too, the Daimler Motor Syndicate was formed by the incorporation of Gottlieb Daimler's engine patents for Britain (held since 1893 by Frederick Simms) into the empire of Harry Lawson, the man who foresaw and hoped to monopolize the motor car industry. The Lawson syndicate acquired a factory (previously a cotton mill) in Coventry, also occupied by the Great Horseless Carriage Company which was another part of Lawson's exploitation of the market. Coventry Daimlers were built from 1897, largely on the Panhard et Levassor system. Daimler himself was on the board, briefly and nominally, but for long enough to allow his name to go with the product. British use

BELOW *Typical voiturette (the usual term for any early small car): the pioneering firm of de Dion-Bouton made its first steam vehicle in 1883, so had considerable manufacturing experience when it built this petrol-driven car at the turn of the century. Many early de Dion-Boutons are seen on the annual London–Brighton Run, reflecting the large numbers built.*

LEFT *Billancourt, Paris, 1899: Marcel Renault is the passenger in the de Dion quadricycle; brother Louis is at the controls of the prototype (de Dion-powered) Renault; Paul Hugé drives the new 'production' Renault on the right.*

BELOW *No history of the motor car is complete without a tribute to Panhard and Levassor. They established the new means of transport in familiar bonneted front-engine, rear-drive layout in 1891, as in this 1902 10 hp Panhard.*

of 'Daimler' is, however, misleading: it is not related in any way to Daimler or Benz, *or* Daimler-Benz! This tends to obscure the fact that many Coventry Daimler cars are classics in their own right.

Monopoly was also rife in the United States of America. It was a forward-looking nation, of course; but it was so vast that it was difficult to imagine a self-propelled vehicle travelling between cities on the terrible roads. Mechanization of the roads would come—but would steam, electricity, or some other form of motive power predominate?

Many patents were established, but No 549160 is the one that stands out historically. Patents take a lot of resolving, and George Baldwin Selden's case was no exception. Selden had made his first application in 1879, but interpretation and modification kept his patent in limbo for no less than 16 years! In that period many experiments were carried out in the United States; yet Selden's patent was, amazingly, ratified in November 1895. It covered 'carriages with internal combustion engines' in a comprehensive manner. Selden was more an attorney than a manufacturer and, although the Selden car was never a serious market contender, it was to take the strength of Henry Ford to trample it to death.

The new century

With the 20th century came the establishment of the classic marques and, during the first five years, the motor car finally became accepted.

Speed became an important factor, and once again France was in the forefront. The first fight for the world's land speed record was held during 1898 and 1899, between Count Chasseloup-Laubat and Camille Jenatzy of Belgium. The count used a modified touring car built by Charles Jeantaud, who wanted to promote sales of his Paris taxicabs. The count established a record at Achères, near Paris, in December 1898. From then, alternately until the next spring, he and his challenger pushed the record up from 63.15 to 105.88 km/h

(39.24 to 65.79 mph). That record stayed with Camille Jenatzy (whose car, *La Jamais Contente*, was, like the Jeantaud, streamlined in an elementary way and powered by electricity) until 1902, when one kilometre was covered in less than half a minute for the first time ever. This was achieved by the Léon Serpollet steam car on the famous Promenade des Anglais, Nice, increasing the record by some 15 km/h (9 mph). Two years later, Henry Ford himself managed more than 145 km/h (90 mph) but in the same year, 1904, Louis Rigolly in a Gobron-Brillié passed 100 mph for the first time—166.65 km/h (103.55 mph)—for France (although he achieved this in Belgium). The classic cars made in France before World War I are almost innumerable; but perhaps they are typified by the Gobron-Brillié, a car of innovation *and* high quality, yet destined to be a victim of the changed trading conditions of the 1920s.

But it was Panhard who reigned supreme in those early days. ('Levassor' remained in the company title, but not in the marque name.) It may not have been greatly significant that Panhards won hollow victories in the first two poorly supported Gordon Bennett Cup races of 1900 and 1901. However, a Panhard also won Britain's first important sporting competition, the 1900 Thousand Mile Trial, and the driver was the Hon. Charles Stuart Rolls, who was later to co-found Rolls-Royce. Other foreigners to win major events in Panhard cars included Britain's Charles Jarrott and the American George Heath. In fact, Panhard's 'performance' image soon declined, and was not helped by the introduction of smoky sleeve-valve engines in 1911, which were slower and less efficient; none the less the marque continued to surprise the motoring world for many a year.

Peugeot also remained consistently strong, despite a family split that resulted in the shortlived Lion-Peugeot. Renault's progress in the industry was meteoric and, before war came, output was more than 10,000 cars a year. Today Renault is a leading Grand Prix contender; back in 1906, too, it was a Renault car, with sloping nose and characteristic bulkhead-mounted radiator, that won the first ever Grand Prix near Le Mans.

De Dion-Bouton never sustained its initial momentum as a company, so Darracq took over the reputation of being able to produce cars quickly and cheaply. Citroën had not yet burst upon the scene, but Delage, Delahaye and Hotchkiss were moving forward as typically French marques of sporting type. Other great names of early motor racing, such as Brasier, de Dietrich and Chenard-Walcker, would not last the pace for quite as long.

The greatest of *all* French racing cars did not appear until shortly before World War I. Born in Italy, Ettore Bugatti won his first design prize at a Milan exhibition in 1901, when he was 20 years old. Baron de Dietrich, who was looking for ideas, saw and liked Bugatti's. In 1902 the young Italian

LEFT *Regular production of the smooth-running Lanchester, a pioneering British marque, began in 1900. This 1904 model has its engine between the front seats: hence the singular appearance of these very original cars.*

BELOW *By the early 1900s, most cars had steering wheels rather than tillers. Herbert Austin (left of picture) with one of his later Wolseleys: he left that firm in 1905 to found his own famous make.*

moved to de Dietrich's Alsace factory. Later, after a period with Deutz (of 'Otto' fame) Bugatti began applying his own brand of perfectionism to car manufacture—not only to cars of his own, but also a miniature car, the *Bébé* Peugeot of 1912. However, his greatest cars were to come after the war.

Elsewhere in Europe, the classic marques were establishing themselves. In the south, precision of manufacture and elegance of line mark the Hispano-Suiza as Spain's greatest car of all, its lack of national competition not detracting in any way from its place as an all-time 'great'. Its creator, in 1904, was Marc Birkigt, a Swiss railway engineer whose attention to detail even led Rolls-Royce to obtain agreement to use certain features. Birkigt's aero engines were to be among the finest available to the Allied forces in World War I. From 1911, Hispano-Suizas were made in Paris as well as in Barcelona.

In Italy, FIAT made some fine cars for touring and racing. Indeed, Vincenzo Lancia and FIAT probably made the fastest competition driver and car combination of the 1905–6 period. In 1907, Felice Nazzaro's FIAT became the first foreign car to win France's premier race, the Grand Prix. However, Lancia left FIAT to put his name and inspiration into a car of his own in 1906.

Alfa Romeo – a classic and evocative name – came soon afterwards. Anonima Lombardo Fabbrica Automobili started manufacturing cars in 1910, in a Milan factory formerly used to make French Darracqs. Nicola Romeo joined five years later, hence the name Alfa Romeo.

Apart from FIAT, the most famous car in Italy in the first decade of the 20th century was the fast, tough, orthodox Itala. It must have seemed the ultimate in motoring when Prince Borghese and his crew used one to win the original 'Great Race'—the Peking to Paris trial of 1907. Like so many fine race-winning Italian marques—the Ceirano-inspired SCAT and SPA cars for example—the Itala did not survive into the era of modern car making; ironically it may have been a renewed attempt at motor racing that later brought about the company's demise.

Germany's industrial scene had begun to take a more definite shape at the first Berlin motor show in 1897, when the latest products of Benz and Daimler were joined by a somewhat Benz-like vehicle built in Dessau by Friedrich Lutzmann. The Opel brothers, already in the cycle and sewing machine business, wanted to make cars—quickly—so they bought the Lutzmann 'system' and in 1898 put the Opel-Lutzmann into production. It did not sell well enough, so, in 1902, they bought a Darracq design from France before gaining sufficient experience to go their own way. Opel made many fine cars of all types, from the smallest to heavy machines of more than 10 litres, progress pausing only when fire destroyed much of the Rüsselsheim factory in 1911. (Since 1928 Opel has continued under the wing of the American firm, General Motors.)

Eisenach and its castle, the Wartburg, gave their names to two new German cars of 1898, one being a Decauville design from France. Once the company had become sufficiently confident, the Fahrzeugfabrik Eisenach renamed its cars 'Dixi' (Latin for 'I have spoken', implying 'the last word on the subject'); and indeed those early Dixis were luxurious and of high quality.

It is not possible to mention every one of the motor industry's minor classics, long forgotten through the demise of a company, a change of direction, or simply a lack of development. Even the adoption of a revolutionary engine design in more recent times seems to have been insufficient to give the NSU marque classic status; yet, back in 1889 when it was known only as a knitting machine and cycle manufacturer, the Neckarsulmer Fahrradwerke provided the chassis (basic framework) for the 'steel-wheeled carriage' built for the 1889 Paris World Fair by Maybach and Daimler.

The Benz marque, after its brilliant start, was to have a chequered history. The founder moved away to work with his sons, and later Benzes were the work of others, notably Hans Nibel whose monstrous Blitzen ('Lightning') model was to take the world's land speed record by brute force in 1909–10,

culminating in a run at 228 km/h (141.7 mph) at Daytona in Florida.

Germany's big leap forward as a nation producing great cars was the result of the enthusiasm of an Austrian millionaire. Diplomat, banker, businessman Emil Jellinek was a 'small excitable man' who reminded historian 'Bunty' Scott-Moncrieff of Toad of Toad Hall. Jellinek loved cars, and persuaded Maybach and the Daimler board to make a new sporting model, guaranteeing the first year's sales. While this project was blossoming, Gottlieb Daimler died and his son Paul—no mean designer himself—went to Wiener-Neustadt to join the new Austro-Daimler company.

'Jellinek' might not have made the ideal name for a car; but the wealthy benefactor had daughters. The younger one was called Maja, and a four-cylinder car of that name was built at the Wiener-Neustadt works in the 1907–8 period. The elder daughter's name, Mercédès, was to become a household word—for it was borne by the Bad Cannstatt cars from 1901 onwards. The sporting style of Emil Jellinek was echoed effectively by great drivers like Camille Jenatzy, who won the 1903 Gordon Bennett Cup, and Christian Lautenschlager, twice winner of the Grand Prix (1908 and 1914). In the years immediately before Europe was engulfed by war, the Mercedes star was in the swiftest ascendancy. The Mercedes was in effect the modern car, so it is hardly surprising that Benz declined to some extent.

In Wiener-Neustadt, the marque name Austro-Daimler was retained (apart from the Maja) for Austria-Hungary's leading make. Ferdinand Porsche took charge of design in 1906, when Paul Daimler returned to Germany. However, Porsche was not the only advanced thinker in Central Europe, and the Nesselsdorf works benefited from the presence of both Edmund Rumpler and Hans Ledwinka in the early days. (Nesselsdorf, the town, became part of Czechoslovakia after World War I and was renamed Koprivnice; Nesselsdorf, the car, became the Tatra, which is discussed later.)

Switzerland has never been prolific in car making, but it did produce a classic 'white elephant' in the 1905 Dufaux with its enormous 26.4-litre engine. Early Dufaux cars were made by Piccard and Pictet in Geneva. Their own first car, the 1906 'Pic-Pic', was a Marc Birkigt design, featuring great precision and workmanship.

In industrial Belgium there were cars galore, the early classics being Excelsior, Métallurgique, Miesse (steam cars, also built in Britain) and, most famous of all, Minerva. The Minervas were magnificent cars that, from 1908, used the Knight sleeve-valve engine to remarkably good effect. The Hon. C.S. Rolls sold Minervas in the United Kingdom, and it was a Briton, Lord Brabazon, who gave the marque its first big race win in the 1907 Circuit des Ardennes in Belgium.

Across the border in the Netherlands by far the most important of the early 'greats' was the Spijker (usually spelled Spyker to assist foreigners), a noble machine that gained fame in the 1950s as the steed of the late Kay Kendall and Kenneth More for their duel with 'Genevieve', the Darracq, in the film of that name.

The Scandinavians produced several early cars, and indeed the oldest car ever to run on British roads is thought to be the restored 1887 Hammel, which completed the 1954 London to Brighton veteran car race and is the pride of Denmark's Tekniske Museum at Elsinore.

The quest for excellence

To make 'The Best Car in The World' has been the dream of

LEFT *It did not take much to turn a touring car into a 'racer' in the early days. This example is a 1905 model from de Dietrich, a company that originally made its name with railway locomotives. The second seat was for the accompanying mechanic.*

BELOW *Engineered by a Swiss, Marc Birkigt, and built in Barcelona (later also in Paris), the Hispano-Suiza marque was much admired. This 1912 15T model was called the Alfonso, because of the patronage of King Alfonso XIII of Spain.*

many an engineer, but who is to be the judge? The consistent claim to that title by Rolls-Royce has remained convincing, if only for the lack of serious challengers. Charles Stuart Rolls was looking for good cars to sell when he met Frederick Henry Royce and saw the 1904 prototypes Royce had built. Royce made electrically operated cranes in Manchester, and decided to construct his own cars for two reasons: one was the failure of his second-hand Decauville to start on the day he bought it in 1902, and the other was the desirability of putting to good use some under-utilized factory space and labour.

Rolls and Royce made a great partnership, despite an age gap of nearly 15 years, but it took a third man, Rolls's colleague Claude Johnson, to organize the business. Quality and performance were plain for all to see when Rolls was runner-up in the 1905 Isle of Man TT and won it the following year. After a brief look at a V8 design, and determined to reach the wealthiest customers with the best possible product, Johnson, Rolls and Royce introduced their regal 40/50 for the London motor show of 1906. This smooth, silent 'six' had a capacity of 7 litres and was later given the name 'Silver Ghost' by Johnson, who also pushed through the one-model policy which was to establish the 40/50, and therefore the Rolls-Royce, as simply the best.

Rolls, more and more enthusiastic about flying, left the company in 1910 only to be killed in an air crash. Royce was in failing health, but continued to design aero engines, and it was Johnson's presence that ensured Rolls-Royce's survival and prosperity. He promoted Rolls-Royce continually: in 1911, a modified 40/50 was driven from London to Edinburgh in top gear averaging about 11.77 litres/100 km (24 mpg)—an exceptional figure, doubted by some—and gave its name to one of the finest of Rolls-Royces, the 'London-Edinburgh'.

This achievement may have been the final nail in the coffin of Britain's first prestige car, the Napier, which had only recently made the same run without managing 20 mpg. It was even noted that the Rolls-Royce was the slightly faster car, although Napier had always been known for speed. Back in 1898, cycle-racing enthusiast Selwyn Francis Edge had asked Montague Napier to modify his Panhard car for him. D. Napier and Son Ltd of London had a fine reputation for the accuracy of its coin-weighing machines, and this engineering quality shone just as brightly when the firm began making cars in 1900.

Edge was the company's leading promoter, and he made Napier Britain's first internationally successful racing car when he won the 1902 Gordon Bennett Cup—albeit through the failure of others rather than sheer speed. Pace came later when in Florida in 1905 Arthur Macdonald became the fastest man on land at 168.48 km/h (104.65 mph). Shortly afterwards, in England, Clifford Earp came close to 160 km/h (100 mph) on the Madeira Drive, Brighton, using the same car. Those first Brighton speed trials were run from east to west, and the story of Earp's efforts to stop before reaching the Palace Pier became a legend—as did the car itself, L48, nicknamed 'Samson'. A reproduction of this magnificent car was being constructed in Australia in the early 1980s. From 1906, Napier concentrated upon touring cars.

The Coventry Daimler was becoming very British in character, assisted by royal patronage. It remained unstable financially, and was probably saved by becoming part of the Birmingham Small Arms (BSA) group in 1910. By that time Daimler was committed to a policy of fitting the Knight sleeve-valve engine, which emitted gentle blue smoke trails —as anyone who has seen early films of royal motoring must

ABOVE *The commercial classic: the Ford Model T, or 'Tin Lizzie', was introduced in 1908, and this one dates from 1910. Production exceeded 10,000 in 1909, 2 million in 1923, and over 16.5 million had been made when the type was phased out in 1927. Only the VW 'Beetle' has bettered this record.*

LEFT *The Gordon Bennett Cup events were succeeded by Grand Prix racing from 1906 (Renault was the first GP winner). This huge 1907 Itala sets the whole scene. The marque's most famous victories were, however, in the 1906 Targa Florio and the 1907 Peking to Paris race.*

RIGHT *American pioneer: Frank Duryea at the tiller of his own make, about to win America's first organized motor race—the snowbound* Chicago Times-Herald *event—in November 1895. Duryea's president George Hewitt stands behind the car. The passenger is a race 'referee'.*

know—but also ran with an oily smoothness. Besides engineering, elegance—not speed—was the hallmark of Britain's Daimler. The company's work on tank and aero engines, ambulances, trucks and a whole variety of munitions work kept Daimler's Coventry factories active throughout World War I.

In its early days the British motor industry in general did not produce many true classics. Daimler, Lanchester, Napier and Rolls-Royce were the most obvious 'top-drawer' cars. However, shortly before those with suitable facilities switched to war work, Vauxhall joined the élite with the Laurence Pomeroy-designed 'Prince Henry' and 30/98 models. Displayed at the 1911 motor show, the Prince Henry can be considered Britain's first true sports car, and was called after Prince Heinrich who gave his name to a series of trials in which Vauxhall was successful.

American beginnings

While Europe's established car makers used their skills to create materials for the European war, North America's new industry was concentrating on business wars of its own.

Henry Ford must be mentioned first. He built a car at home in Detroit in 1896, and created the Ford Motor Company in 1903. His first classic was the 'Tin Lizzie', the Model T, with its unorthodox transmission of only two forward speeds, which meant a special driving test for owners. The 'T' was introduced in 1908, and its low price and high production rate made it the universal car, keeping Ford at the top of the manufacturing tree for 19 years.

The Selden patents, referred to earlier in this chapter, probably had little long-term effect on the American car industry, but much time and energy were expended on their account in the courts. It was Ford who in 1911 finally broke down the barrier by showing that the patent could relate only to a particular two-stroke engine; by that time most manufacturers were using four-stroke units anyway. By then, too, the curved-dash Oldsmobile, the first mass-produced car of all, was already history. This car got its name from its buggy-type body, which curved up at the front as a footrest. Made by Ransom Eli Olds, it became America's best-selling car in the 1903–05 period, with around 5000 manufactured in 1904. Later Olds left, his former company moved into the mid-price bracket, and Ford took over market leadership.

There were American cars that never stood a chance of survival and others that became absorbed into the new groups. Classic makes that will not appear in later chapters include Chadwick, the first to employ supercharging—where air is forced into the cylinders by a 'blower'—to improve performance; Christie, who anticipated the transverse engine and front-wheel drive of the British Mini by more than 50 years; Duryea—the Duryea brothers were the first Americans to run a car on the road with an internal combustion engine; Peerless, luxury car makers who turned to brewing after Prohibition; Pennington—E.J. Pennington was the classic con man who probably produced fewer cars than he had companies to make them; the Pope Group, which failed when Ford succeeded; Stanley, whose steam car smashed the world land speed record in 1906; and White and Winton, two makers who tried so hard with their motor racing.

The war in Europe dragged on. The next great age of motoring would not begin until 1919.

RIGHT *'Prince Henry' Vauxhall, 1911–14, with characteristic bonnet fluting. Its successor, the 30/98, brought even more fame—GM's take-over changed the character.*

INSET *The world's first mass-produced car, before even Ford, was the curved-dash Oldsmobile runabout: a classic of simplicity. This one dates from 1903. Annual output reached 5000.*

V 2948

TRUE VINTAGE

French flair: art and automobile combine in the late-1920s 8-litre 'Boulogne' Hispano-Suiza (PRECEDING PAGES)*, the Kelsch-bodied Delage DIS tourer* (ABOVE) *and the Bugatti Type 37* (RIGHT). *The last-named was the sports car adaptation of the Type 35 GP model (it is seen here during a modern retrospective event).*

The terms 'classic' and 'vintage' are generally used in too loose a way. The latter is, in fact, quite precise when applied to cars as opposed to wine. In its earliest days, Britain's Vintage Sports Car Club selected the 12 years from 1919 to 1930 inclusive as its period of interest. Undoubtedly, this was an era of particularly fine cars.

If the motor vehicle had once been unfamiliar to the man in the street, this was definitely not the case by Armistice Day in November 1918. Thousands of men and women had witnessed the first mechanized war—whether at the front or in the factories and flax fields of home.

The internal combustion engine had ensured the practical development of the aircraft and the tank, although neither was strictly ready for combat in the early campaigns of the war. Cars were adapted for military use; the French moved their troops in the Marne campaign with the aid of scores of commandeered taxis.

Motoring for the masses had not yet arrived; at least not in car form. The motorcycle and sidecar was still the more fortunate family's personal transport in Britain. The lightweight, generally low-powered cyclecar and voiturette had grown from the even spindlier motorized tricycles and quadricycles of pre-war France, which had well over 300 registered car manufacturers. The immediate post-war boom, followed by recession, would slash that figure by more than 80 per cent. The big got bigger quickly and the weak went to the wall, or switched to a less risky industry.

While the variety of marques decreased, the availability of the car to a wider public became a fact. There is a place in this book for the popular marques that set major trends; but for the most part the classics of 1920s and 1930s came from the specialists whose engineering or business skills—or both—enabled them to survive on merit for long enough at least to establish a reputation.

French style

One effect of war was the production of smooth-running, high-performance luxury cars resulting from aircraft experience. The classic example in France was the Voisin, produced at Issy-les-Moulineaux aerodrome where the first model was tested early in 1919 and, it is said, went backwards

instead of forwards due to wrong assembly of the transmission—a tale of uncertain authenticity that has also been told of the first Volvo. All Gabriel Voisin's cars, like his aircraft, bore the stamp of eccentric genius. They were carefully styled for space or streamlining, and those made in the vintage period had Knight sleeve-valve engines, including V12s. Voisins appealed to enthusiasts, because one of their maker's preoccupations was precision and lightness in the controls.

Hispano-Suiza had become more French than Spanish by the 1920s and the factory at Bois-Colombes, which was ideally located to take advantage of the great French coachbuilders, rapidly gained its reputation as the country's finest car maker. The performance given by the 6.5-litre, six-cylinder, alloy-block overhead camshaft (ohc) engine made it necessary for Marc Birkigt to improve stopping power by pioneering four-wheel brakes with gearbox-driven servo-assistance for the H6B which starred at the 1919 Paris Salon. Its specification seemed to outdate even Rolls-Royce's 'Silver Ghost', with which it vied for the 'best of all' title at the time.

Blériot, Farman, Fonck and Gnome et Rhône were probably even more famous in the world of aviation. Only a few cars of the latter two makes ever reached customers, and Blériot cars do not come into the 'classic' category. On the other hand the Farman, which lasted from 1920 to 1931, had many of the Hispano-Suiza's characteristics. It was a touring car of outstanding quality; it had a big overhead camshaft straight-six engine behind an equally imposing radiator grille, and it had four forward gears—one more than on the Hispano. Both were doomed, but the Farman failed with the vintage years. Even near-perfection is no guarantee of survival. (Rolls-Royce, it is to be hoped, is an exception to the rule.)

French sports cars of the old school provided home victories in three of the first four Le Mans 24-hour races, which were created to promote roadgoing machines, to the extent that four seats and ballast in place of passengers had to be carried. Chenard-Walcker won once and Lorraine-Dietrich twice. Ettore Bugatti, his Alsace premises having been occupied by the Germans, spent the war in Paris as an aero-engine designer; on returning to Molsheim his productivity and ingenuity knew no bounds, and by the late 1920s his Type 35 was consistently the leading Grand Prix car. The fabled Bugatti Royale of the late vintage period failed because of the

Depression, but fortunately the company lived on.

Ballot and Delage were France's other two leading racing car makers of the decade. Ernest Henry of Switzerland, who had designed Peugeot's pre-war competition engines, provided Ballot with a superb power unit with twin overhead camshafts and four valves per cylinder. Ballots swept to a one-two victory in the first Grand Prix of Italy in 1921. Mechanical works of art were trademarks of Delage, too. After Delage's none-too-successful 2-litre V12, engineer Albert Lory designed a superb and reliable straight-eight, low friction, 1.5-litre supercharged engine (with more than 60 ball and roller bearings). This unit produced 170 brake horsepower (bhp) and gave complete superiority to Delage in the 1927 season. Delage would have been given the manufacturers' title had there been one. Likewise, the leading driver, Robert Benoist, certainly deserved his *Légion d'Honneur*; there was no 'world champion' title then. The GP formula changed for 1928, and the cars were sold; but Delage also managed to develop a fine line of touring cars throughout this period, and the marque's claim to 'classic' status is as worthy as any.

Hotchkiss and Panhard did not have quite the distinction of Hispano-Suiza in the vintage years, but remained sufficiently sporting and interesting to keep going as other great pioneering names—de Dion was, perhaps, the saddest example—slid to their fate.

Market leaders Peugeot and Renault did not make the mistake of falling behind the times, and they also maintained a successful sporting presence. The straight-eight 7.1-litre Reinastella of 1929 was the first Renault for years to have its radiator in front of the engine. It was also the most luxurious

BELOW AND ABOVE RIGHT *The late-vintage variations of the Tipo 8 Isotta-Fraschini were dream cars—and not only in the advertiser's eye. Their like has not been seen again (except in an abortive 1947 revival).*

RIGHT *Italy's most successful sports car of the late 1920s was the Alfa Romeo 6C model, with a 1.5-litre overhead camshaft engine designed by the great Vittorio Jano. Continuity for the Alfa Romeo marque was ensured by nationalization.*

Renault of all time; its predecessor, the 45, fails to pass muster as a classic on the grounds of its antiquity at the time of its introduction (it even had wooden wheels). On the whole, though, France of vintage times was pre-eminent in engineering variety and originality, in dash and style, as it had been when it had led the world into car building.

Italian grace and speed

Vintage Italy too had its Grand Touring car, and it stood out from its compatriots in a most commanding manner. In 1919 Cesare Isotta and Vincenzo Fraschini announced their intention to follow a one-model policy; and, just like the Rolls-Royce, their new car would be the ultimate in silky, silent travel. The engine was low-powered but it was the first practical production straight-eight in the world and the torque was such that the wide ratio three-speed gearbox seemed an unnecessary extra when the car could be set in motion in top gear so easily! (Torque is the usable power available at the crankshaft. It is a measure of turning or twisting effort, most simply experienced when starting from rest with a bicycle.) The 6-litre Tipo 8 was replaced after five years by the 7.4-litre Tipo 8A and the more sporting Tipo 8A 'SS'. With the SS ('Super Spinto'), Isotta-Fraschini promised 160 km/h (100 mph) without loss of docility. The best export market for the cars was America. What did it matter if these characteristics rarely made the car a race winner any more? Was it not reasonable to trade on past successes if the product was Italy's very best, and modern, too? Of course it was reasonable—until the Depression came.

Itala had already scaled down its products. In 1924 the 2-litre Model 61 was introduced, and it was a very fine touring car, but it did not sell well. Soon afterwards front-wheel drive, supercharging, and a V12 engine for racing were all examined but not followed up. The Itala died with the vintage era.

FIAT was not only the universal car maker of Italy. Like most of the world's mass producers, the company made prestige models from time to time. One of its first post-war offerings was a big 7-litre V12 chassis, but it was withdrawn quickly; FIAT claims a maximum of five built.

The make that typified vintage Italy was quite different. Alfa Romeo of Milan was rapidly becoming synonymous with sporting and competition cars. The firm's great test driver, Giuseppe Campari, gave Alfa Romeo its first big road race win at Mugello in 1920. He also provided its first Grand Prix win, in the 1924 French GP at Lyons; in fact, that was the first *Grand Epreuve* in which Alfa Romeo had ever taken part.

Vittorio Jano came from FIAT in the mid-1920s and was responsible for those superb Alfa Romeo vintage sports cars: the twin overhead camshaft six-cylinder supercharged 6C 1500 of 1928 and the 1750 of 1929.

Before World War II, Maserati of Bologna did not have quite such an automatic claim to classic status, for these cars were born of Italian Diatto out of French Clément: but then there are few good cars that do not have a hint of French flair about them, even if it is hidden by generations of development. The Maserati brothers began making their own cars in the middle of the vintage period, and before the end of it these cars were winning the important races.

Although Vincenzo Lancia's performances for FIAT earlier in the century had singled him out as one of the best drivers of the heroic age of motor racing, his own cars did not figure in

the competitions of the vintage years in the spectacular manner of Alfa Romeo and Maserati. It is, nevertheless, to Lancia that we should look to discover Italy's most significant contribution to the vintage years; for in 1922 his company introduced the first car to combine chassis and basic body in one unit. This feature, combined with independent front suspension and a compact V4 engine, made the Lancia Lambda's specification begin to read like a modern car. Such an audaciously successful design eclipsed comparable Italian makes such as Züst, and its successor O.M., or the vintage Ansaldo and Bianchi, excellent as they all were.

Central and North European vintage cars

The combined talents of Willy Stift and the three Gräf brothers produced a strong vintage contender for the title of top car in Austria: the straight-eight, 6-litre Gräf und Stift SP8. After all, this had been the royal make; the Archduke Franz Ferdinand was murdered in one at Sarajevo in 1914. From the mid-1930s, however, the name was to survive only in the commercial vehicle world.

Top designers kept Austro-Daimler to the forefront. Ferdinand Porsche introduced the ADM type before leaving in the early 1920s; his successor Karl Rabe was responsible for the ADR a few years later. In the late vintage period, Hans Stuck dominated the European hill-climb scene with his immensely powerful Austro-Daimler sprint car, and he introduced the name to Britain effectively in 1930 when he broke the Shelsley Walsh hill-climb record.

In view of the restrictions and difficulties imposed upon it as the defeated nation, Germany did well to provide the classic vintage merger in 1926, following several years of cooperation between Benz and Mercedes. Mercedes-Benz lived up to its two names, on the race track and in the market place. Before long, Mercedes-Benzes were known as the fastest touring cars and racing cars in the world. The SSK and SSKL models were big and immensely powerful, and were to provide the impetus for Germany's success in GP racing in the post-vintage years.

With such a lead, Mercedes-Benz dominated its German rivals, with the exception perhaps of Maybach, a new marque name. Wilhelm Maybach, Gottlieb Daimler's associate of the old days, had joined Graf Zeppelin to make airships. These had engines designed by Maybach's son Karl who, in 1921, began making his own brand of super car, the ultimate being (from 1929) Germany's first V12-engined car.

Another extraordinary machine, a classic in its way, was Edmund Rumpler's 1921 Berlin Show exhibit: a centrally steered saloon, streamlined as a result of his aircraft experience, although it did look more like a boat. The engine was in the back, which had swing-axle suspension (independent suspension but with no means of controlling the wheels vertically). Rumpler continued to experiment but was unable to get many of his own creations into production. Streamlining and the independent swing-axle suspension were taken up by Benz with its teardrop racing car, and that experience was carried through to the Mercedes-Benz marque.

In 1923, Gottlieb Daimler's son Paul joined that pioneering German firm, August Horch of Zwickau, and set it on its luxury straight-eight route with a 3.1-litre twin overhead camshaft model. V8s and V12s would follow. In 1928, another traditional German manufacturer, Stoewer, also began making a series of splendid eight-cylinder models. (The Stoewer factory was in Stettin and after World War II it found itself in Poland—and in ruins.)

Considering how Belgium suffered in the war, it is amazing that so many new luxury cars appeared there in the early 1920s, from Excelsior, Métallurgique and, of course, Minerva.

LEFT *The strange little Hanomag 2/10PS was known as the* Kommissbrot *('army loaf') because of its shape. In the 1924–8 period the Hannoversche Maschinenbau AG made over 15,000 of these 500 cc single-cylinder rear-engined cars. The* Kommissbrot *was too basic to live for long, but it was a classic idea and a forerunner of the German 'people's car'* *(see page 40).*

In the Netherlands Spijker lasted only until 1925, but in Scandinavia a small motor industry was beginning to emerge. Denmark was too tiny to make cars in quantity, and its quality car makers merged to concentrate upon trucks and buses. In Norway, assembly from mainly American components produced the Lycoming-engined Norsk Geijer. It was in Sweden that the motor industry gained its first substantial Scandinavian foothold. Several tentative efforts there were put in the shade by the combined efforts of a new group, helped by the ball-bearing manufacturers Svenska Kullagerfabriken (SKF) and other big companies, which was determined to establish its own quality standards and not to follow others. 'We develop and we improve, but we do not invent' was to be the motto of the worthy Volvo company.

British performance and luxury

England and Scotland made their own big impact on the vintage scene. Scotland is given its own special mention here, for it produced several really good cars. The Beardmore combined solidity with excellent performance which, in 1925, resulted in a new Shelsley Walsh record. The Argyll and the Arrol-Johnston were probably Scotland's best (and best-known) makes: the latter bowed out in 1929 with the sleeve-valve Arrol-Aster straight-eight, which was offered with a supercharger.

In England, the progress of Rolls-Royce typified the immediate and artificial post-war boom. In 1919 a Rolls-Royce engined aircraft made the first trans-Atlantic flight; later that year it was announced that an assembly plant for Rolls-Royce cars would be set up in the United States.

By following Hispano-Suiza as soon as possible with four-wheel braking, and by introducing modern accessories such as an electric starter, the ageing Rolls-Royce 40/50 kept its premier position. The one-model policy could not go on for

LEFT *The last word in German sports cars of the vintage period: the immensely powerful 1928 supercharged 7.1-litre overhead camshaft Mercedes-Benz SSK (short-chassis super sports). Rudolf Caracciola made his name in variations of this model.*

ABOVE *Restrained coachwork from Stabilimente Farina tends to obscure the advanced design of this late model (1930) Lancia Lambda, the first car with integral construction of chassis and basic body. The original version of the Lambda had been introduced back in 1922.*

long, once the economic realities of the 1920s became evident, and towards the end of 1922 a 'small' Rolls-Royce, the 20, was announced. This could be bought as an open tourer for £1590—considerably less than the 40/50 chassis alone.

Ultimate luxury went one stage further in 1925 when the 7.7-litre overhead valve New Phantom was introduced to replace what then became known as the Silver Ghost. Soon afterwards the motive force of the company, Claude Johnson, died suddenly. His successor was an ex-Napier man, Arthur Sidgreaves. He brought out an updated Phantom, the II, in 1929, and this model was supplemented by the magnificent Continental Phantom II, which was approved by Royce himself at his Sussex retreat in the summer of 1930. The lower chassis of the Phantom II permitted coachbuilders to create near-perfect harmony of line, and there were silence and performance to match.

Napier simply could not keep pace in what was in any case a very small market sector. S.F. Edge, promoter of Napier, had left before the war. Fortunately the company now commanded tremendous respect in the aero-engine field, and so the failure of the car to regain its former glory meant that post-war car development in this area was stopped at an early stage. It should not be assumed that there were no labour problems in those days; strikes at Napier's foundry and at its associated coachbuilding house, Cunard, contributed to the marque's final demise in 1924.

Some years later, Napier hoped to return to car making by acquiring the Bentley company, but the bid was to fail. 'Bentley' is the name most closely associated with the word 'vintage'—perhaps with 'classic' too.

Walter Owen Bentley, an aero-engine designer, and former importer of French DFP cars, had drawn up his first chassis in 1914, exhibited it at the 1919 London show (with a dummy engine), and finally delivered one to his first customer in 1921.

Frank Clement gave the Bentley No 1 its first race victory at Brooklands that year, and the Great British Sports Car was born.

The original 3-litre, four-cylinder Bentley went on to win the Le Mans 24-hour race in 1924 and 1927, and the legend was completed by Woolf Barnato's hat-trick of 1928–30: his first victory was with the enlarged 4½-litre model (still a 'four'), and the last two with the magnificent 6½-litre Speed Six, a model derived from Bentley's frontal attack on the Rolls-Royce market. Quick fame and success (or, more likely, a preference for first-class engineering over basic market research) took Bentley Motors into a problem area with Britain's most massive car. Up to this time, Barnato cash had helped keep open the Bentley factory doors; that six-cylinder 8-litre Bentley of 1930 merely hastened their closure.

There were classic oddities among the British vintage exotica in the brief boom period. Best known is the Leyland 7.3-litre straight-eight. Engineered by the eccentric Welsh racing driver Parry Thomas and clothed magnificently by the newly formed British (as opposed to Belgian) Vanden Plas company, it was—with a price tag of over £3000 and an output of nearly 150 bhp—the most expensive *and* powerful car of 1920. No wonder fewer than ten ever appeared. (Now, Leyland's successor, BL, uses the coachbuilding name Vanden Plas in much the same way as Ford uses 'Ghia'—to create 'top models' by special equipment and decoration, rather than by the craftsmanship of the vintage era.)

LEFT *A 1927 4½-litre Bentley, meticulously restored. Bentley cars won the Le Mans 24-hour race five times.*

BELOW *The Rolls-Royce Continental Phantom II appeared at the end of the vintage era—in fact this example with Park Ward coachwork comes just outside it. But what elegance and style!*

Also very expensive was the new Lanchester Forty, developed from the Sporting Forty of 1914. The second brother, George Lanchester, introduced a more conventional layout for his family's marque, but still it possessed traditional Lanchester quality, performance, and inventiveness. The 6.2-litre, six-cylinder, overhead camshaft engine was mated to a three-speed epicyclic gearbox (involving toothed wheels meshed to a flat ring-like structure called an annulus), and silent running was aided by a worm-drive rear axle (based on the screw-thread principle). The Forty was followed in 1929 by the Thirty, a 4½-litre straight-eight with an orthodox four-speed gearbox. This splendid car was the sad swansong of the independent Lanchester.

As a marque name, Daimler was wholly British, and the large Coventry factories had done wonders in the war effort. Not all of the revived Daimlers were of royal car size, but all remained wreathed in wisps of oil smoke throughout the 1920s, for the British company still committed itself exclusively to the Knight sleeve-valve engines. The range was ridiculously broad for a company in the luxury car market, and the introduction of a 7.1-litre V12—the 'Double Six'—brought the 1927 selection of Daimler chassis and engine combinations to more than 20.

Vauxhall continued to improve its 30/98, possibly the highest-geared grand tourer of its day but a major contributor to the company's drastic survival policy, namely the sale to General Motors in 1925.

To tell the complex tales of Sunbeam, Talbot and their French connections lies beyond the scope of this book. However, as individual marques they must be commended. Georges Roesch's finely engineered Talbots, culminating in the 105 model, showed how a good car can have potential performance built in from birth. Sunbeam's fame came from

motor racing and record breaking, for its touring cars were not high performers. Nor, for that matter, was the excellent Armstrong Siddeley from Coventry, fine and imposing as it was with its classically angled radiator grille surmounted by a Sphinx.

Britain led the way in sports car design, and (as can be found in the last chapter) AC, Alvis, Aston Martin, Austin, Frazer Nash, Lagonda, Lea Francis, M.G., Morgan and Riley showed there was a sustainable British market for fun cars to suit all pockets—a market that the post-vintage slump would fail to crush.

A car for the people

Mention of Austin must lead to the story of the British people's classic car. After a feud with the directors, Herbert Austin had left the Vickers-controlled Wolseley company to make his own cars in 1905. The most extraordinary vehicle to bear his name up to (and during) World War I was, however, a truck which looked rather like an overgrown tinplate toy, with its coal-scuttle bonnet and its radiator mounted behind the engine in Renault style. The cargo platform could be as low as 760 mm ($2\frac{1}{2}$ ft) from the ground because of the ingenious, if impracticable, use of two propeller shafts, one to each pair of rear wheels from a central differential unit; ahead of this, the engine and gearbox were inclined down and rearwards, to get the drive-line low. The rear axle was a simple beam. But for a favourable report, following army manoeuvres on fairly easy terrain in the English Midlands, the project would not have been followed up. As it was, the vehicles were made in quite large numbers—probably about 2000—only to be proved unreliable in war conditions. Besides the British order, a large quantity went to the Imperial Russian Army, but an order for 1000 was cancelled in 1917, as a result of the October revolution.

The tale of the growth of the original Austin company is a classic one, and his 2–3 ton truck is just one example of the bold steps Herbert Austin was prepared to take. The ability of his company to adapt to munitions work was rewarded with large-scale expansion, and a knighthood for the founder.

With costly mistakes like the lorry, which was soon dropped from the civilian market, and a post-war one-model policy, Austin soon ran into financial difficulties. That one model was the Twenty, which Sir Herbert Austin believed combined the best of American production techniques with Edwardian quality and could be sold in large numbers at a low price to keep Britain's biggest car factory, at Longbridge near Birmingham, operating profitably. Post-war production difficulties meant fewer cars and higher prices; then came the slump and a drop in demand.

Sir Herbert Austin was not only an exceptional businessman, able to recover his company from the receiver; he was also ready and able to change his policy and design new products quickly. Chief contributor to the rescue of his company, and to a revolution in British motoring, was his Austin Seven of 1922.

This really was a miniature version of the orthodox car. Not a cyclecar or voiturette, it was a cheap 'proper' car, with four wheels, four cylinders and four seats. Also, it did not have

chain drive or a motorcycle engine. Production soared to an annual figure of over 20,000 by 1927 and stayed at that level for more than a decade. From that year, overseas manufacture of the Austin Seven began: the first deal was with the Gotha railway wagon company, whose excellent but rather staid Eisenach-built Dixi cars were not doing well enough for survival. Built under licence, the Austin Seven did not save the Dixi marque, but it did provide a basis for the BMW. When the Munich-based company acquired the Eisenach works in 1928 in order to enter motor manufacture, the German Austin Seven became the BMW-Dixi! In France, Rosengart took up the Austin design; later there was a less successful American Austin Seven, the Bantam; and Datson (later Datsun) undoubtedly copied it in Japan. No other car design since the early days of Benz and Daimler in Germany, or Panhard and de Dion in France, had been so freely adapted abroad.

From the outset the Seven appeared in competitions, and from 1929 there was a supercharged sports model.

The price of the Austin Seven came down as production went up. No manufacturer could yet compete. Triumph was never a serious contender with its Super Seven of 1928, and the company opted for a more sporting market in order to stay in business. The true competitor with Sir Herbert Austin in the vintage period was William Richard Morris. A bicycle dealer and engineer, he had opened a garage in Oxford and given the city's name to his first 'bullnosed' car in 1913.

An assembler, initially, rather than a manufacturer, Morris watched the Austin Seven progress but did not confront it directly until the end of the vintage period. Meanwhile he helped Cecil Kimber—by letting his M.G. (Morris Garages) become the sporting Morris—and bought the bankrupt Wolseley company.

LEFT *The special 1929 lowered-chassis Double Six 50—an attempt at a sportier image for the Daimler. This impressive drophead by Corsica soon replaced the original Weymann saloon body.*

ABOVE *The Austin Seven did not pretend to be anything other than what it was—but, in all its simplicity, it inspired many other designs. This example is a Chummy and dates from 1930.*

American giants and classics

The United States provided European companies with much of the inspiration to build up their production in the 1920s. The activities of American companies then were very varied. The growing conglomerates did make classic cars, but there were some fascinating independents too. The Ford Model T continued to amaze the world until 1927, by which time a remarkable 15 million 'Tin Lizzies' had been made not only in America, but also in Britain and Germany. The Model T's successor, the A, was another Ford to reach the pockets of the people, thanks to its efficiency, its orthodoxy, and its Lincoln styling.

Lincoln had been bought by Ford in 1922, but was to remain a prestige marque in its own right. Europe would learn a great deal from the American marketeers. Years earlier, the founder of Lincoln had been responsible for another great name in American luxury motoring: Henry M. Leland, a colleague of Henry Ford's, back in the earliest days of the American car, had formed the Cadillac company in 1902.

The early Cadillac was conventional enough, but gained recognition in Britain in 1908 when three cars were assembled from a pile of parts and then driven rapidly round the Brooklands circuit. The make became part of General Motors in 1909, and the first V8 Cadillac appeared in 1915. Fifteen years later Cadillac hit the headlines again with the first series-production car to have a power unit with sixteen cylinders.

General Motors was the brainchild of William Durant, a business brain and not a technological expert like David Dunbar Buick, the Scottish-born inventor whose cars were noted for their use of overhead valves from the outset. Buick was no organizer, and the company that had bought him out in 1904 put in Durant, who had made a fortune from the carriage trade. In 1904, Buick had made fewer than 50 cars; in 1905, thanks to Durant, 750 had been built.

Durant's dream was to tie up the American car industry, as Lawson had tried to do in Britain earlier. Durant was more successful, however, and although he failed to bring in Ford he had registered General Motors in September 1908. By the 1920s, Durant was taking risks of staggering proportions. As a result the Du Pont corporation took over his shares, and General Motors went on to become the world's biggest car maker, consisting of Buick, Cadillac, Chevrolet, La Salle, Oakland, Oldsmobile, Pontiac and other lesser marques. The Oldsmobile curved-dash runabout may have been the original mass-production buggy when the new century had started, but Cadillac was to be the American super car in the long term. In 1928, Cadillac's 'clashless' gearbox introduced a grateful world to synchromesh, where gears could be changed smoothly. Before, if the engine revs were not judged precisely, the gears could only be engaged with difficulty, often resulting in 'crashing' noises; thus the term 'crashbox'.

Victory in classic motor races helps create classic cars, but it seems only too easy to forget this in the case of American products. How many Europeans cared to take note of the unknown marque that won the Grand Prix of France—home of the motor car—in 1921? It is true to say that it was one of the all-time surprise victories of international motor racing, when Jimmy Murphy beat the Ballots to win convincingly in what was in effect the first Grand Prix car to have hydraulic brake operation: the Duesenberg.

Fred Duesenberg and his brother August had been putting their skills to good use for a long time, but did not give their own name to them until 1920. Following Murphy's Grand Prix win, Duesenbergs won the Indianapolis 500-mile race four times.

The most successful Indianapolis car of the 1920s and 1930s was the Miller, which gave power to the first successful Duesenberg and went on to win the race 12 more times! Harry Miller's cars were usually racers; but he did make a remarkable V16 sports car in 1932, at the time of his bankruptcy.

The most exclusive car of vintage America was the Cunningham, which is not connected with the 1950s sports car of that name. James Cunningham of Rochester, New York, made a beautiful V8-engined 6-litre touring car beloved of the Hollywood fraternity. More famous among America's top vintage cars was the Pierce-Arrow. Acquisition by Studebaker in 1928 seemed to help the make, for nearly 10,000 were made in 1929. Then sales dropped once more and in the early 1930s efforts were being made by devotees to rescue the marque.

Studebaker deserves mention alongside America's classic cars,

Two great American vintage sporting cars: Stutz was successful in competitions at home and in Europe. One came second at Le Mans in 1928; this example (BELOW) *was made soon afterwards. The Cord* (RIGHT)*, not a competition car, had de Dion-type front suspension and front-wheel drive. The L-29 was made in small numbers in 1929–32.*

if only for longevity. Studebaker wagons had first rolled in 1852; an electric car came 50 years later, but America's oldest name in vehicle making was to die in 1966, despite interesting styling and several attempts at revival. Packard, another great name in its day, was to join forces with Studebaker in 1954 and vanish ignominiously soon afterwards, despite having been the world's first 12-cylinder car maker and the first world land speed record-breaker of the vintage era.

The 1910–30 period in America produced keen rivalry in the sports car market, Mercer and Stutz being the main contestants. The Mercer was just too specialized, and the company folded in 1925. Stutz lasted into the 1930s, and obtained an excellent reputation at home and abroad, particularly after one of these cars ran a strong second to Bentley at Le Mans in 1928. Third and fourth in that race were two more American high-performance cars, Chryslers. It was in that year that Dodge, pioneer of the all-steel body, joined forces with Chrysler to become the USA's third largest motor group. Soon afterwards, the fine Chrysler Imperial straight-eight was launched to challenge Ford's Lincoln and GM's Cadillac. The Imperial appeared to borrow its style from the 1929 Cord L-29.

Errett Lobban Cord already had Auburn, Duesenberg and Lycoming under his wing, but the car bearing his name was something quite new. It was long and low and yet well-proportioned. It had a straight-eight Lycoming engine and Harry Miller's patented front-wheel drive featuring de Dion type *front* axle. For a brief period the Cord L-29 found it had a rival in the front-wheel drive Ruxton, of which only a few were made before the collapse of New Era Motors—the combination of Kissel, Moon and Ruxton.

In the United States, as in Europe, survival into post-vintage years would call for tenacity. What hope was there for the air-cooled Franklin and the Doble, the greatest of all the steam cars, if some of the best of the orthodox vehicles were fading out of the picture? The answer, regrettably, was none!

Nowadays such machines would be called dinosaurs. Nevertheless they were magnificent cars, created by brave and imaginative people; and, thank goodness, that is how they are remembered today, and why many are preserved.

CARS FOR EVERYONE

The term 'classic' is not restricted to expensive cars produced in small numbers by specialist manufacturers. The mass-produced Ford Model T and Austin Seven were examples of truly pioneering classics that helped to make the car an everyday item for increasing numbers of people—a process that really got under way in the 1930s.

The 1930s were a time of great uncertainty for many nations, beginning as they did with the great Depression when so many companies went bankrupt. However, some of the finest luxury and sports cars ever seen were produced in this decade. Because the big manufacturers were competing desperately for custom the car became much more refined and, by the mid-1930s, real sophistication was part of the everyday motoring scene.

Besides its 'Big Three'—Citroën, Peugeot, and Renault—France produced domestic versions of the FIAT and Ford under the names 'Simca' and 'Matford'; the latter title indicated the end of the Mathis marque.

Peugeot and Renault avoided taking serious risks with their everyday models, and it was André Citroën who took France's biggest technological stride forward when he launched his new *traction avant* (front-wheel drive) car in 1934. It was a design that would not be altered radically for 22 years and still inspires engineers around the world. At the time it nearly finished Citroën financially. The most popular model was the *Onze Légère* (11 hp), also built in Britain as the Light Fifteen (15 hp): French horses were obviously stronger than British ones!

The *traction*, as it is generally known, was not the world's, nor even France's, first car to have front-wheel drive. Like all novelties it had imperfections, but when it worked it worked well. Front-wheel drive has a number of advantages, including the elimination of transmission to the rear wheels; this saves weight and provides more room in the passenger area because the propshaft tunnel running down the centre is no longer necessary. In the 1980s, this system is virtually universal in small and 'family' cars (the Ford Sierra is a notable exception). Thanks to the Michelin tyre company, Citroën cars continue to be made today, and still show great individuality. Back in 1934 the new cars bristled with modern features like unit construction of body and chassis, designed so that all the mechanical components could be wheeled out from the front for major servicing. The main feature of the independent springing was the use of torsion bars, a means of controlling the twisting forces between the sprung and the unsprung parts of a car. The Citroën was the first car to bring the terms 'ride' and 'handling' into everyday motoring; and through the Michelin takeover it provided a free test-bed for modern tyre development. Much of the Citroën's stability came from having 'a wheel at each corner' (i.e. the wheels were as near as possible to the front and rear of the car, thus spreading the load over a bigger area). This was a big factor in yet another extraordinary Citroën feature—its timeless styling.

While Citroën was becoming a world leader, the designers of the revered Panhard seemed keen to step backwards. Panhard, too, used unit construction for its Dynamic of 1937; but it retained the oil-guzzling Knight double-sleeve-valve engine—the last make to do so—and had the most outrageous and unharmonious appearance. The driver sat in the middle of this extraordinary 'plum pudding' of a car that was certainly expensive enough to warrant inclusion in the chapter on luxury cars, yet too weird to qualify otherwise. It is mentioned simply to show that long experience does not necessarily prevent marketing mistakes. World War II came in time to

save the grand old name of Panhard further embarrassment.

Italy and Central Europe: economy and ingenuity
Turning to other European countries, it becomes clear that Spain was no longer producing any early classics. The monarchy was lost and the country plunged into civil war.

In 1936 Italy, however, came up with two of the most outstanding economy car designs ever. Like Renault, FIAT tried to cater for every single motorist, lowly or lordly. The tiny two-seater *Topolino*, as FIAT's new baby was dubbed, was the world's first completely new miniature car since the Austin Seven. The FIAT Tipo 500A had a small four-cylinder engine ahead of the front wheels, and its styling was endearing in the extreme. A year afterwards it was complemented by the family-sized *Millecento*, another very attractive model but less advanced than Vincenzo Lancia's final offering—final because he was to die shortly after the announcement of his Aprilia.

The Lancia Aprilia was a compact and light four-door saloon that followed the Citroën in having its wheels as near as possible to its extremities, torsion bar suspension, and a modern (although less attractive) streamlined body. The Aprilia also marked a return to unit construction in which Lancia had played a pioneering role with the Lambda. It had an excellent performance and, like the Citroën, was appreciated in Britain where well-behaved family cars of advanced design were as yet unknown.

By the mid-1930s Austro-Daimler, Puch, and Steyr had merged. From 1936, only the Steyr name remained. In that

PRECEDING PAGES *The Series E Morris Eight, introduced in 1938. Note built-in headlamps.*

LEFT *Rare open version of the 1930s* traction avant *Citroën.*

BELOW *Peugeot's late-1930s 402 models echoed the Chrysler Airflow's streamlined look but without such ugliness. This sporting version by Darl'Mat did well at Le Mans.*

year, too, Dr Porsche gave Austria its only true 'people's car' in the Steyr 50. Streamlined, with front styling not unlike the FIAT 500, this interesting little machine had a horizontally opposed, water-cooled four-cylinder engine at the front, driving the rear wheels through swinging axle shafts, a simple suspension system but one that allows considerable change in the wheel camber, thus reducing roadholding ability. Swing axles, pioneered in Rumpler and Benz projects of the 1920s, were characteristics of Hans Ledwinka's Tatra designs for the top end of the Czech market, in which there was considerable competition between half a dozen small-car manufacturers.

A German people's car evolves
Germany's first attempt at a people's car had been the Hanomag 2/10 PS of which over 15,000 had been made when Dixi brought out its own version of the Austin Seven, built under licence in Eisenach from 1928. In the same year a Danish engineer, Jørgen Rasmussen, gave birth to the most significant of early German small cars, the DKW (the initials stood for *Dampfkraftwagen,* German for 'steam car', and reflected Rasmussen's early work with these vehicles). Already well known in the motorcycle field, DKW set a trend in design-for-economy in 1931 with its front-wheel drive, two-stroke, twin-cylinder miniature. Rasmussen was also involved in Audi and, therefore, in the formation of Auto Union in 1932. Soon afterwards, that collective name was applied to Porsche-designed Grand Prix cars, but the DKW name was retained for the small cars throughout the 1930s, and again after World War II. Rasmussen's basic front-wheel drive, two-stroke concept was used by others including Jawa in Czechoslovakia, and lived on (after the DKW name died) in more modern times in the Swedish Saab and, less happily, in several East German guises.

In 1931 the little Dixi was being transformed by its new owners, the Bayerische Motoren Werke. BMW's chief designer, Fritz Fiedler, was quick to modernize the Dixi so that its Austin background was soon virtually unrecognizable. As the BMW name succeeded Dixi, so the new marque moved quickly away from economy vehicles to sports cars.

On a par with BMW and DKW for design in the 'popular' sector was the front-wheel drive Adler Trumpf-Junior—a creation of Hans-Georg Röhr, following his resignation from the company bearing his own name. Developments in Hitler's Third Reich included the new German road system—the *Autobahnen* ('motorways'). It is noteworthy that some 1500 km (nearly 1000 miles) were in use well over 20 years before the word 'motorway' meant anything to Britons! One result of these new roads was the adoption of streamlining for fuel efficiency on many everyday German cars, including the Adler, Hanomag, Hansa, Zündapp and finally—just before World War II—the Volkswagen.

In the late 1930s the Volkswagen of course was far from being 'everyday', even though it was later to become the world's most popular car with over 15,000,000 made. Indeed,

RIGHT *Rather like the FIAT* Topolino, *especially in looks, the Steyr 50 and 55 of 1936–9 were Austria's only true 'people's cars'. Over 12,000 of these front-wheel-drive economy cars were built. The Type 50 had a 1000 cc water-cooled four-cylinder engine. Its successor, the 55, had 1150 cc and some 25 bhp.*

BELOW *The 1931 DKW F2 front-wheel-drive two-seater from Germany. With a 600 cc two-cylinder two-stroke engine, this Jørgen Rasmussen design was Northern Europe's most popular small car for nearly a decade.*

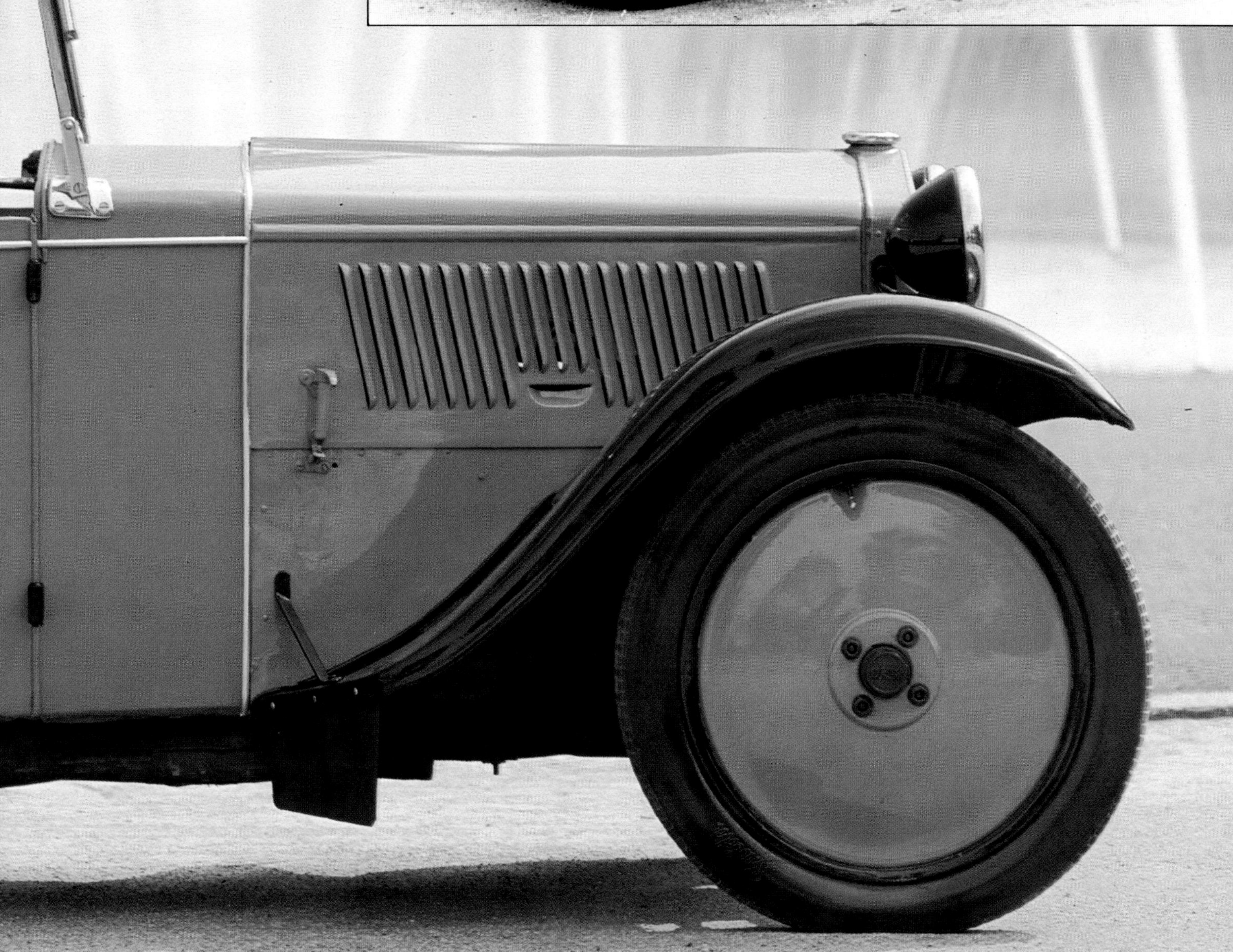

Wolfsburg, Lower Saxony, 26 May 1938: when he laid the foundation stone for the factory, Adolf Hitler, with three of Ferdinand Porsche's prototypes before him, announced that the 'people's car' would be called the KdF-Wagen. *This change from the agreed* Volkswagen *name would have made no sense in export markets. However, VW civilian production did not start until 1945, under Allied control. The 'Beetle' is still being made (in Brazil). The total numbers produced are over 20 million—figures that have long since passed those for the Ford Model T, the previous record-holder.*

in the mid 1980s, the VW 'Beetle' is still being produced in Brazil and could become the only car to remain in production 50 years after it was first created.

It could be said that the VW had its origins in the Austro-Hungarian empire even though it was made in Germany.

Several famous men are involved in the story. Josef Ganz, who designed the rear-engined Gutbrod Standard Superior of 1932, was Hungarian. No one will ever know how much the design of his aerodynamic rear-engined, independently sprung little coupé influenced the VW as we know it. Earlier, when he was a German citizen, Ganz had been a journalist, and as far back as 1928 had advocated the introduction of a really cheap car, which he had described in print as a 'German people's car' (*Volkswagen*). He used this term again to advertise his Standard Superior, which Hitler and his entourage reputedly examined in detail during their official tour of the Berlin motor show early in 1933, shortly after the new Chancellor's appointment. It was not long before Ganz's chances of being appointed to design a government-backed project evaporated when he was identified as a Jew and imprisoned. Fortunately he was freed and escaped to Switzerland.

However, the most important man behind the VW was Dr Ferdinand Porsche. In the early 1930s he worked as an independent engineering consultant, based in Stuttgart, and in 1934 Hitler's chief motor industry adviser Jakob Werlin summoned Porsche to meet the Chancellor in Berlin to discuss a national car project. Not long afterwards, he was contracted to the German car manufacturers' association (RdA) to produce three prototypes. After these were completed by a team working in Porsche's double garage, a pre-production run of 30 *KdF-Wagen* was undertaken at the nearby Daimler-Benz factory. *KdF-Wagen* was the name announced by Hitler when he visited the chosen factory site in Lower Saxony in 1938; it stood for *Kraft durch Freude*, or Strength through Joy, which was a Nazi movement responsible for organizing 'leisure' pursuits and was presumably used because it was thought that the German people should have wider access to motoring. The public, however, was not able to buy the 'Beetle' until after the war, when VW production began in earnest under very different circumstances.

The battle for the £100 car

'Island' Britain lived up to its reputation at the start of the 1930s: it did not look far beyond its shores for ideas. Long-distance motoring was not a British occupation or pastime, as the design and maintenance standards of its roads made all too clear.

However, there was still a wide choice open to the British motorist; but among the cheaper cars, the imports were not regarded as much of a threat to the home-built products. As on the continent of Europe, American cars were quite popular in Britain, but there were no small ones available. Even Ford's smallest car, assembled in Manchester, had an engine of more than 2 litres and cost nearly £200 in 1931.

At that time, in its tenth year of production, the Austin Seven could be bought for just over £120. The Morris Minor with overhead camshaft engine was only slightly more expensive but, as William Morris's own sales director Miles Thomas acknowledged, it was a 'troublesome baby' and did not sell as well as the established Austin; so Morris made a change, simplifying the specification by turning the engine into a side-valve unit and by offering an absolutely basic model for only £100!

This little Morris Minor two-seater tourer was announced in January 1931 and, as at least one newspaper pointed out, 'Four years ago this same car could not have been produced for twice the price.' It was not a sudden drop in price, however, that made it such a success; it was the clever marketing. People were demanding value for money and would pay 20 to 30 per cent more for a comfortable four-seat saloon or cabriolet (convertible) variant if the price of the basic model was (say) £100! 'No one wants to keep down with the Joneses', observed Miles Thomas later, when he and Morris were members of the peerage.

It was America, not continental Europe, that brought the truth home to the British motor industry. Having invested in a huge new plant at Dagenham on the north bank of the Thames, Ford's finances were not noticeably affected by the renting of London's Albert Hall for a private motor show. It opened on 19 February 1932 and one of the first visitors was Sir Herbert Austin, who was as keen as anyone to see the car that was to ensure a permanent presence for Ford in Europe.

The Ford Y-type was American in concept if not in scale. It was longer and wider than the Austin Seven and Morris Minor saloons, but only by enough to make it a full four-seater. Soon it was in production at £120. Austin responded in 1934 with the Ruby, which was still really the old Seven, but Morris went a stage further, copying the 'baby' Ford unashamedly with the Morris Eight. Singer did the same with the Bantam, but brilliant production engineering enabled Ford to drop the price of the Y-type or Popular saloon to a genuine £100 and peg it there for 1936 and 1937, before bringing in a new version at just under the old price of £120.

The British road tax system was based on an artificial 'horsepower' directly related to the cylinder diameter or bore; this encouraged the use of long-stroke engines which could provide increased power output without affecting the Treasury's horsepower rating. Modern engines tend to have dimensions that are roughly 'square'—that is to say, with similar dimensions for the bore (or cylinder diameter) and the stroke (the distance travelled by the piston in the cylinder). The longer the stroke, the deeper the engine.

The horsepower rating for the Morris Minor and the Ford Y-type was 8 hp, although the latter was nearly 100 cc greater in swept volume—the space displaced by the travel of the

BELOW *Neutral Sweden was able to start its post-war programme ahead of most of the car-producing nations, so Volvo's PV444, launched in September 1944, was the first definitive new European car of the 1940s. So successful was the design that the basically similar and perennially sporting PV544 remained in production 20 years later, still bringing Volvo worldwide acclaim. This PV444, with period 'extras', is in use today.*

piston multiplied by the number of cylinders, which today is the recognized way of describing an engine's size. When Morris wanted more power without putting its new 'Eight' into a higher tax bracket, the company simply copied the Ford's long-stroke design.

Morris and Austin had half the UK car market between them in the early 1930s, but Ford's share was soon up to 20 per cent. The late 1930s saw a general acceleration of production and increased sales for cheaper cars from makers who had been skilful enough to survive the Depression. Standard and Triumph had not yet merged but still seemed healthy, producing small cars only slightly more expensive than the cheapest Austins, Fords and Morrises. Second-in-command and aspiring leader of the Standard Motor Company of Coventry was John Black, and he knew that the typical small British car was dull and old fashioned—a situation maintained largely by British conservatism.

Birth of the Jaguar

Another man to see the need to bring style to British motoring was William Lyons. He had been selling glamorous, good-value Swallow sidecars to war-weary enthusiasts since 1922, and from 1927 had been offering brightly painted luxury coachwork for the simple Austin Seven. The Swallow company had been so successful that Lyons moved it south from Blackpool to Coventry in order to make use of local manufacturing skills and to expand.

Standard soon became a chassis supplier to Swallow, whose individual styling began to give the firm a reputation for coachbuilding. But Lyons could not achieve the sleek low-line styling he wanted on any of the chassis available to him. In 1931, however, he persuaded Black to supply him purpose-built chassis. The result was the SS—both men avoided putting words to the initials—and Lyons had a marque of his own. For four years SS style was not supported by useful performance. In 1935, however, Lyons recruited William Heynes, a young engineer from the Humber company, to set up an engineering department, and between them they created the SS Jaguar car. The envious gave the new marque rude names, but history has shown Lyons, who was later knighted, to have been one of the car industry's most astute businessmen.

To the colleagues Heynes left behind at Humber, SS Cars may then have seemed a small outfit of no great consequence; but Heynes had felt restricted, nor had he liked what was happening. Humber had been among the pioneers of Coventry's motor industry; the cars, however, were well made but dull. Also, the Rootes family became involved, taking a major stake in Humber and its neighbour Hillman.

Badge engineering

The Rootes empire as such does not have a place in this chapter, except for a passing mention of its various marketing activities. These put it among the big manufacturers, adding Sunbeam and Talbot to its collection of marque names and bringing American-style 'badge engineering' to Britain. This is a method of dressing up models with different badges and trim to give the impression that a new car has been produced, or that a marque still has an independent existence after being taken over.

The expansion of Morris Motors into the Nuffield Organization was more gradual and carefully handled. The Wolseley marque, begun by Herbert Austin in the 1890s, before he had struck out on his own, was rescued in 1927, and kept alive as a luxury Morris. Riley managed to avoid capture until 1938; then it too became a member of the Nuffield group. (Sir William Morris was now Lord Nuffield.) During this period Vauxhall lost its character under the General Motors banner. The old order was changing, yet mechanical invention was singularly lacking in Britain throughout the decade. The Austin Seven became overgrown and outdated, and small German cars such as the DKW were becoming available at reasonable prices; but the Third Reich was more and more being recognized as an enemy. Buying British became simply the most natural thing to do. Citroën anglicized its 1935 front-wheel-drive models, and made them in Slough in Buckinghamshire. The servicing might have been expensive, but a more advanced car could not be bought in the very competitive price range of £200 to £300.

The 'popular classics' of the 1930s cannot be dismissed, however, without reverting to America's dreams and skills. In

ABOVE RIGHT *Its underslung chassis and skilful styling gave the 1934 SS1 saloon distinctive, sporting lines at bargain price. The required improvement in performance came with the first SS Jaguar range in 1935.*

LEFT *The £100 car achieved: the Morris Minor with side-valve engine was announced in January 1931, pared to bare essentials at £100. Not everyone wanted so spartan a car: the more fully equipped Minors at around £125 sold better. Ford's Y-type, 1932, looked modern and offered more space and performance. This 1936 model* (RIGHT) *dates from when the type was sold as a complete car for £100. Morris unashamedly copied this Ford from 1934 to '38. Then came the Morris Series E (see photograph, pages 36-7).*

CHP 127

1934, Ford's 'baby' was supplemented in the UK by its new V8 model. At a mere £225 it brought eight-cylinder motoring to the masses, although at a British rating of 30 hp, the annual tax bill of £1 per horsepower must have seemed enormous. In fact, from 1935 the tax went down to 15 shillings (75 pence) for a few years, but the system remained and Ford brought out a 22 hp V8 to ease the situation.

War and the aftermath
Britain may have been at the top of the quality league (see next chapter), continental Europe the mother of invention, and North America the leader in mass-production techniques, but from the outbreak of World War II in September 1939 the whole world changed, and the manufacturers had to turn their attentions to military production.

In the USA it was possible to make cars for the public well into the 1940s. Although most American cars were big by the standards of other countries, there was one important exception. The brainchild of Powell Crosley, whose talents had previously been applied to the manufacture of radios and the patenting of refrigerator designs, the Crosley car introduced in May 1939 was designed to be manoeuvred through a department shop door so that it could be sold alongside other products of this manufacturer. It was shown at New York's Grand Central Palace motor show in 1940 and soon afterwards in Macy's department store. Despite its economy and many inventive features, the Crosley survived only a few years into the post-war period and was not able to compete with Willys as the greatest American small car producer. Even the Austin Seven had been a failure in the United States, as was its successor the Bantam. In 1940 the American Bantam company was commissioned to make a light military car, but was unable to produce it in quantity. Over 650,000 military Jeeps were manufactured—the majority by Willys Overland but many,

also, by Ford under contract. The Jeep was of course a landmark in automobile history and lives on in several forms around the world as a result of licences sold after the war.

When war did end in 1945, production began again tentatively in the victorious nations. Russia took enough equipment from General Motors' German plant to make its own version of the Opel Kadett, calling it the Moskvitch. In Britain the early post-war models were mostly revamped pre-war types. In some cases failure would probably have been avoided had brand-new designs been adopted. But those who dug among the ruins—like Alvis and Lea-Francis in the heart of Coventry—never succeeded in modernizing their product enough to offer anything really new. On the other hand Jaguar and Rover already made very attractive cars, and these would see them through until their new models came along. The highly reputable Rover moved out of war-torn Coventry, but SS Cars (renamed Jaguar Cars Ltd because the initials also stood for the hated Nazi formations) stayed put. John Black had wanted to join William Lyons's board but, unable to gain admission, bought the failed Triumph company on behalf of Standard. He was determined to make a Standard-Triumph car that would put Jaguar out of business. Only one of those three marques lives on today.

Before the end of 1945, however, several completely new cars were announced. Amazingly quickly off the mark was Armstrong Siddeley with its rather heavy 2-litre models called after famous British warplanes (Lancaster, Hurricane, Typhoon and Whitley). Soon afterwards came the classically styled $1\frac{1}{2}$- and $2\frac{1}{2}$-litre Rileys—which temporarily rid the marque of its rather staid 'Nuffield' image—and the Jowett Javelin. The latter was a departure for the Yorkshire company, best known for 40 years of economy cars, mostly lightweight twin-cylinder models. The Jowett Javelin, announced in 1945, was a sensation not so much for its streamlined body and compact flat-four $1\frac{1}{2}$-litre engine with horizontally opposed pairs of cylinders, but more for unit construction and torsion bar suspension, which gave the car handling to match its excellent performance. It is ironic that Jowett would be one of many companies never fully to recover.

Late in 1945, *The Light Car* magazine reported 'Some 3000 workmen are engaged on the production in Germany of the KdF, for officials and the occupation Forces.' In today's terms, the rear-engined, swing axle layout seems permanently outdated. It may have cost VW dearly, when the company tried to update the original concept before successfully switching to front-wheel drive; but if the KdF, the much-loved 'Beetle', did take Volkswagen down a blind alley it is hard to regard that as a mistake. Of all the mass-market cars, the 'Beetle' must be *the* classic.

ABOVE *Ford achieved a coup in 1932 by introducing the first mass-produced V8 engine. This is one of the original Ford V8 styles. An 'everyday' classic, with mascot, 'sidemount spare', whitewall tyres and speed, it provided Hollywood-style motoring cheaply.*

RIGHT *The diminutive Crosley with its 600 cc two-cylinder Waukesha engine appeared in 1939. Styles included the 'covered wagon': one of these toured the USA at better than 5.65 l/100 km (50 mpg)!*

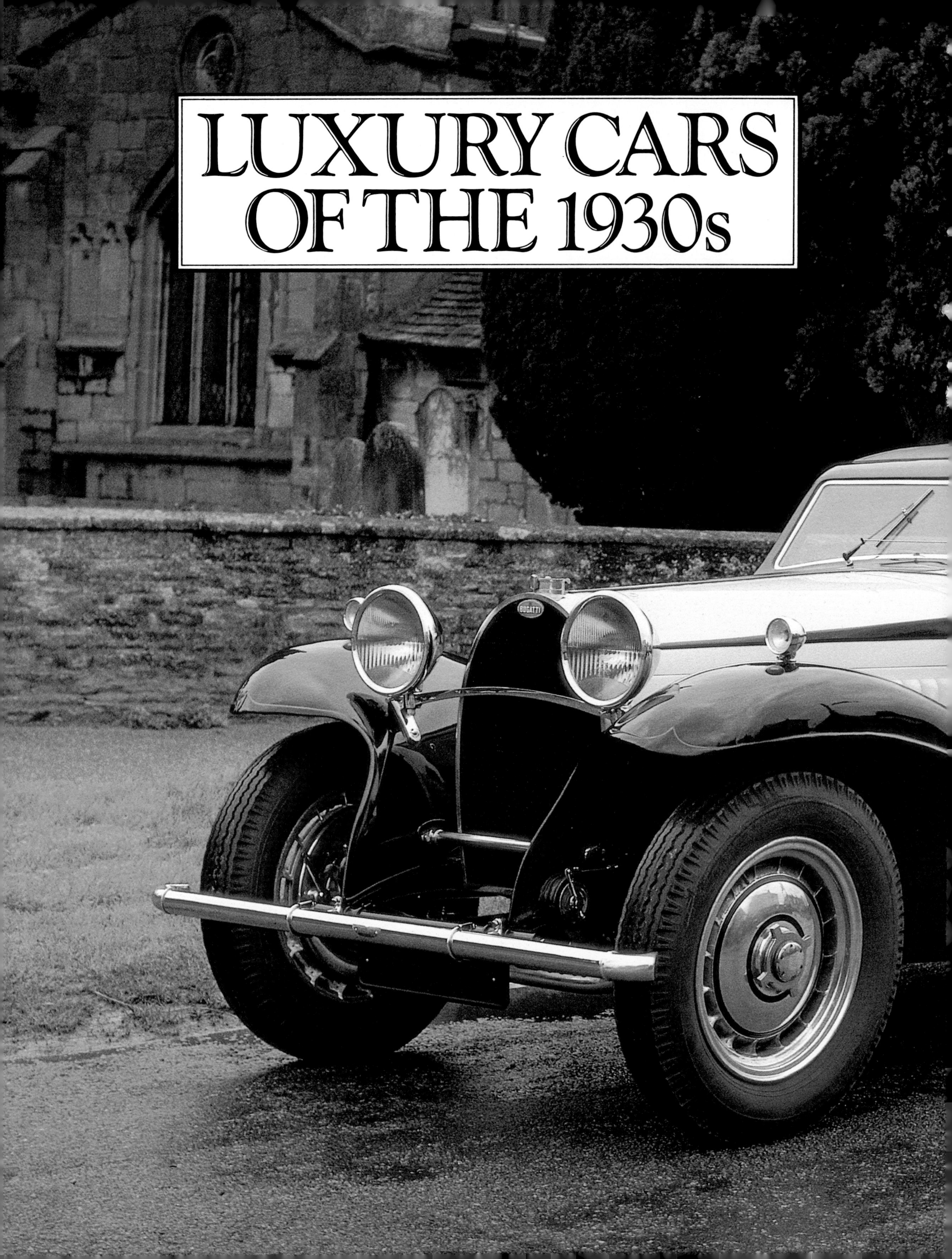
LUXURY CARS
OF THE 1930s

Of all the early classics, the Bugatti stands head and shoulders above the others for a sheer brilliance that remains undimmed by any new research or discovery. The sternest critics could not fail to be impressed by all that Ettore Arco Isidoro Bugatti achieved in the creation of this glamorous marque.

In the spring of 1977, an Alsace textile factory was taken over by its workers. In the course of this action, and much to their surprise, the night raiders burst in upon an Aladdin's cave of over 400 cars. Almost all were classics—122 of them Bugattis! The brothers Hans and Fritz Schlumpf, whose collection had previously been regarded as a matter of fantastic rumour, were already across the border into nearby Switzerland; they had used huge sums of money from their business to buy exotic cars from all over the world, and the warrants for their arrest for embezzlement had come too late.

Their incredible private museum was opened by the workers, then closed again. Since 1982, and now as a French national motor museum, the Schlumpf collection in Mulhouse is open for all to see. However, even this huge collection amassed and hoarded by the two brothers has not harmed the exclusive image of the Bugatti: it remains decidedly uncommon. And had it not been for Ettore Bugatti, it is probable that the cult of collecting great cars might have been less obsessive than it often is.

As mentioned in the chapter on vintage cars, Ettore Bugatti's talents had been applied to the advantage of others before he set up his own business in the Alsace wine town of Molsheim in 1909. By the early 1930s, Bugatti's reputation was spurring him on to even greater achievements than his handful of dream cars, the enormous eight-cylinder 12.8-litre Type 41 Royales, two of which were hoarded by the Schlumpfs. The Royale was simply too big and expensive and became a victim of the economic crisis of those years; but its smaller successors, the Types 46 and 50, were superb luxury machines in their own right. The latter's 5-litre engine was the first of Bugatti's twin overhead camshaft units—inspired to some extent by the great American engineer and tuner, Harry Miller.

The design, presentation, performance and variety of Bugatti's cars justified his continued registering and re-registering as a trademark the catch phrase *Le Pur Sang* ('the Thoroughbred') whenever he could. (One Bugatti advertisement that followed some competition successes actually showed a thoroughbred racehorse. Ettore Bugatti had been horse-mad since he was a boy in Italy, and even the Bugatti works club-cum-hotel was called *L'Hostellerie du Pur Sang*.)

The combination of artist and engineer showed in all Ettore's work, as it did in that of his elder son Gianoberto (usually known as Jean) Bugatti whose eye for elegance of line was expressed in that most beautiful road car the Type 57. This twin camshaft, 3.3-litre car—often supercharged—was the most desirable high-speed touring car of the 1930s; it was usually clothed in bold, brilliant coachwork to the young Bugatti's design, built at the Molsheim works or by Gangloff in nearby Strasbourg. Then Jean Bugatti was killed, testing a car between Strasbourg and Molsheim within a month of the

PRECEDING PAGES *A gorgeous Bugatti T50 of the 1930s.*

LEFT *A 1935 Hispano-Suiza 11.3-litre 68bis V12 (body by Saoutchik).*

ABOVE *Champagne cocktail: a 1939 Delage D6-75, which was the product of an alliance with Delahaye. Both these French marques continued into the early 1950s.*

outbreak of World War II in 1939. The marque never really recovered sufficiently to survive for long in the post-war years, let alone return to its former glory. Ettore himself died in 1947, leaving financial chaos, and his friend Gabriel Voisin remarked unkindly that Ettore Bugatti's car making had been 'merely a game'.

Voisin was a fine one to talk! His 1937 sleeve-valve 12-cylinder in-line engine was ridiculously long, and must have been a jest. No bonnet could accommodate this unit and it protruded into the cockpit of a car which, not unnaturally, never sold. The last few Voisins had orthodox six-cylinder engines supplied from the United States by Graham, but the marque faded as war approached.

As with Bugatti, Voisin styling was sometimes as striking as its engineering was original. This originality (and angularity) was to appear in new, contrasting form when Voisin returned from the aircraft industry to design a miniature post-war utility car, the Biscuter, as a 'mini' car for Spain.

Sadly, that great name Hispano-Suiza would not appear on a car after the war: the Barcelona factory was turned over to truck manufacture by a new company, ENASA. (Later, that modern classic, the Pegaso grand touring car, would be made in what had once been the Hispano-Suiza apprentice school.) The Paris-built Hispano-Suiza had lived up to its reputation during the vintage years when a new 9.4-litre V12 model was announced in 1931. When the capacity was increased to 11.3 litres in 1935, there was no doubt who made 'France's Rolls-Royce'. (Bugatti had no British equivalent.)

Years earlier, the fine engineer and occasional racing driver for Benz, Marius Barbarou, had moved on to design cars for Delaunay-Belleville, arguably France's greatest make before World War I. In the 1930s Barbarou was still contributing to

BELOW *The fine Austrian driver Hans Stuck Snr, seen here with his road-going car, was largely responsible for keeping the sporting image of the Austro-Daimler alive in the early 1930s.*

BOTTOM *Delahayes were excellent touring cars that could win races and rallies. This is the 1936 3.2-litre* Coupe des Alpes *model, predecessor of the famous 135. Coachwork is by Labourdette, some of whose designs were copied from those of Britain's SS.*

French prestige, but his smooth Lorraine—the last product of the de Dietrich concern, where Bugatti had once worked—faded quietly in 1933, the year of the demise of de Dion-Bouton. Delage, however, stayed afloat after being bought by Delahaye in 1935, and those two marques continued in production into the early 1950s, when Hotchkiss took over. Both Delahaye and Hotchkiss were regular Monte Carlo Rally winners before and after World War II. Benjamin Berkeley Hotchkiss was a 19th-century industrialist-of-fortune who made guns for Napoleon III and originally came from Connecticut in the United States. The cars that bore his name never lost their fine reputation; but after 1955 the Hotchkiss company concentrated on commercial vehicles.

The Italian Isotta-Fraschini remained magnificent throughout the 1930s, but sales declined; its great years had been in the vintage era (see the second chapter). The final death throes did not come until the mid-1940s, however, when an ambitious V8 rear-engined model, the Monterosa, failed to find a market.

The exotica of Italy remained largely sporting and are featured in the next chapter. On the other hand, the mammoth

FIAT empire *could* produce worthy 2.5-, and later 2.8-litre, six-cylinder saloons. Lancia's V8 3-litre Astura had a good performance, handled and steered well and, with the Italian coachbuilders' art at his disposal, the well-heeled customer could buy a very nice combination of luxury and modern design. A long-chassis Astura with coachwork by Pininfarina was not exotic, but it looked very elegant indeed in such chic clothing.

In central Europe, there were few super cars in the 1930s—and they were made for state occasions. For a while, Austria had its Austro-Daimler and Gräf und Stift for such purposes. In Czechoslovakia, the Walter aero-engine company offered regal transport, even listing a 5.7-litre V12 model, to supplement the top Skodas and Tatras.

However, Hungary's best car of the day, the M.A.G. Magosix, was worthy but certainly not a classic. In Scandinavia the same applied to the Volvo, although it was maturing impressively. War would affect development, of course, but Sweden's neutrality did permit Volvo to make plans while others were fighting.

German power and luxury

Germany, however, did have some luxury cars. In the late vintage period the industry's oldest names—Benz of Mannheim and Mercedes (formerly Daimler) of Stuttgart—had come together and the new marque, the Mercedes-Benz, entered the 1930s as the epitome of power with the launching of the 770 Grosser ('larger') model. The type name indicated the engine size—7.7 litres. There were eight cylinders in line, and much of the car's appeal came from the use of a supercharger which howled into action whenever the chauffeur engaged the full 200 bhp available under his right foot. This was a formidable machine, but when fitted with well-proportioned coachwork it was as impressive as any car on the market, and as such was favoured by kings and princes. Its chassis design was orthodox, but that was replaced in 1937 by a new tubular one with independent suspension based on that of the spectacularly successful Grand Prix cars. The engine could now produce 230 bhp with the supercharger in use, although this huge car could have done with even more power. Later versions became familiar in their grim official

Two superb early-1930s examples of German grandeur. LEFT *This Type 770 Grosser supercharged, 7.7-litre, straight-eight of 1932 was the exiled Kaiser Wilhelm's last Mercedes-Benz. He had special controls in the rear compartment for signalling instructions to the chauffeur.*

BELOW *Flagship of the new Auto Union combine from 1932: the 6-litre V12 Horch Type 670. This Spohn-bodied cabriolet has the distinctive three-piece windscreen. The amazing rear-engined Auto Union GP cars (page 72) were built in the Horch factory at Zwickau in Germany.*

guise, weighed down by military officers and armour plate.

Less directly reminiscent of the Third Reich was the rare and massive Maybach. When its V12 engine was increased in size to 8 litres in 1931 the name Zeppelin was adopted, a reminder that Maybach made airship engines too.

The Maybach Zeppelin chassis was made on a grand scale, as was the specially built coachwork. An odd Maybach characteristic (also applicable to the early Grosser Mercedes-Benz) was the use of multi-speed gearboxes. Big 'lazy' engines usually make a wide range of gears unnecessary, so the Maybach Zeppelin's complicated transmission with eight forward speeds and four reverse (and three levers to control it) seems rather ludicrous in retrospect. All Maybachs were beautifully made, however, and the streamlined Zeppelin of 1933—inspired by Jaray and built by Spohn—must have been one of the most exciting vehicles designed specifically for the new German motorways.

A rather more realistically priced and proportioned V12 was the 6-litre Horch. However, at Horch, as at Mercedes-Benz, the emphasis was on eight-cylinder cars. From 1932 the Horch was the standard-bearer of the new Auto Union, and its excellent styling rubbed off on its medium-sized colleagues bearing the brand names Audi and Wanderer, while DKW (see chapter three) looked after the small-car end of the combined range. The two-piece windscreen had been familiar for a long time, but the modern curved-glass type was still to come. However, the big Horch of the early 1930s may have created the idea with its three-piece screen—a large centre section plus an angled pane at each pillar. Hupmobile in America and Panhard in France copied the scheme but, of the three, the Horch was by far the most attractive.

The whole of Germany's industry had to start again from scratch in 1945, of course, and was not fully in charge of its own affairs until some years later. Of the classic luxury cars of the 1930s, only the Mercedes-Benz has moved into the modern era to maintain the German tradition of thoroughness and excellence in its designs for production.

In the Low Countries the Minerva alone of all the great classics lived into the 1930s—but a merger with Imperia led only to the assembly of everyday makes from other countries, and subsequently no Belgian car was worthy of the beautiful insignia of the goddess Athene, the famous mascot that graced the front of the Minerva.

Quality from Britain

The social class structure helped to ensure variety in Britain's luxury market. The economic problems of 1931 also helped, in fact, for it was the year of two eminent mergers.

It was thought for a while that floundering Bentley Motors would be taken over by another London firm, Napier, who by then was making aircraft engines not cars. The idea of a Bentley-Napier was conjuring up dreams of speed and excellence when Rolls-Royce made its move and snatched Bentley from under Napier's nose.

In 1929 Rolls-Royce had updated its smaller range by bringing out a new 3.7-litre six-cylinder model, the 20/25. It sold well for a car in the top class; nearly 4000 were made by 1937, and formed the basis for the 'Silent Sports Car'—the new owner's catch phrase for the Derby-built Bentley, launched in 1933. Even into the 1980s, Rolls-Royce was giving the Bentley a distinctly sporting image, to help justify keeping those two great names alive.

Sir Henry Royce was not in good health, and he never saw the great V12 that bore his name: the Rolls-Royce Phantom III which appeared in 1935. He died in 1933, and from that year onwards the overlapping 'RR' radiator lettering was no longer painted red but black. Contrary to popular opinion these two facts are not connected. It was thought that red clashed with certain colour schemes used on the cars.

Combined sales of the six-cylinder Phantoms I and II had been nearly 4000 in the previous decade. In the few remaining years before World War II, just over 700 Phantom IIIs were made. At 7.3 litres, the Phantom III was slightly smaller in capacity than its six-cylinder predecessors, and the early models did not have quite the performance or reliability essential for 'The Best Car in the World'. A new design of cylinder head was introduced in 1938, to give the car over 200 bhp shortly before it became obsolete.

The Phantom III had several advantages, such as independent suspension, but somehow it did not quite live up to its forerunners. A probable reason is that a V-engine configuration with smaller cylinders allows a shorter bonnet than one covering a long straight six or eight. The result was that the coachbuilders could not always provide the Phantom III with quite the right proportions, whereas it would have been difficult to make the earlier Phantom II anything other than lovely. Rolls-Royce and Bentley have weathered many bigger storms than the relative lack of success of the Phantom III, and lived to tell the tale; and that must be seen as a measure of their worth as classic British makes.

The other British merger of 1931 was the more complicated one of Lanchester with Daimler; the latter company had been part of the BSA empire for over 20 years.

Britain's Daimler had been so named in the 1890s as a result of the acquisition of UK patent rights for Gottlieb Daimler's internal combustion engine principle. (Daimler of Coventry never had any connection with the Daimler-Benz company nor the Mercedes-Benz car—which today is the chief rival of Jaguar-Daimler products in the prestige car market.)

The Lanchester, made in Birmingham, had been on a par technically with the Rolls-Royce. The senior Lanchester brother, 'Dr Fred', had adopted the role of consultant—to his own company *and* to Daimler—early in the century. His brother George had been the chief designer throughout the vintage years, and his splendid finale, the straight-eight Lanchester Thirty, was still being offered in 1932.

The Lanchester's future role, however, was dictated by those who may have seen its reputation as a threat to Daimler. Daimler made cars of high quality, but they were also old fashioned and only now was the company prepared to update

its engines under the direction of chief engineer Laurence Pomeroy, formerly of Vauxhall fame.

The first Lanchester to be brought out after the merger was a joint effort by Pomeroy and George Lanchester called the 15/18, and it gained the distinction of being the winner of the first-ever RAC Rally, early in 1932. This achievement was not the result of a sporting performance but more the ability to creep along at very low speed, due to Pomeroy's scheme for combining a fluid coupling between the engine and the gearbox with a preselective feature: that is to say, a gear could be selected in advance by a hand lever, then engaged at will by the left foot, a 'gearchange' pedal replacing the clutch pedal. A similarly equipped Daimler Double-Six came second in that first RAC Rally, while strong clutch-burning smells emanated from the more orthodox cars as they tried to put up a reasonable performance in the crucial slow-running test, better suited to a state procession than a genuine sporting competition, on the promenade at Torquay in Devon.

After its collapse, the Bentley marque was resuscitated by Rolls-Royce as the 'Silent Sports Car'. The sweeping elegance of this $3\frac{1}{2}$-litre 1934 sedanca was provided by coachbuilders Gurney Nutting.

Despite its RAC Rally victory, the Lanchester car would never be the same again, for the new Daimler sales policy was to introduce cheaper ranges of models to stay in business—and the Lanchester name had to fulfil that role. At under £600 the 15/18 was probably good value, but its engine position meant that the radiator was placed well forward; and that made the car rather ugly at a time when the traditional and prominent radiator cowl was a distinguishing feature and an integral part of the individual car.

The Daimler-Lanchester combine adopted Pomeroy's fluid flywheel and preselector transmission system for all its models. None of the new Lanchesters was forced into having a sleeve-valve engine, however, and positive steps were being taken to replace it with what Daimler salesmen called the Silent Overhead Valve power unit.

Its staid image was becoming something of a handicap for the Daimler, and one effort to remove it in the early 1930s was the lowering of two Double-Six (V12) chassis, to which sporting coachwork was fitted. The engineering modifications to these two monsters were carried out by Thomson & Taylor of Brooklands, under the supervision of Reid Railton: he later became famous not only for production cars bearing his name but also for John Cobb's Railton Mobil Special world speed record car.

Even the very last pair of Daimler V12 engines was given overhead valves (the days of the inefficient sleeve-valve unit were over). Those V12s were, at $6\frac{1}{2}$ litres, not quite as large as some earlier Daimler Double-Six units; but the cars were as impressive as any of their predecessors, for they were King George V's 1935 Silver Jubilee limousines—one for him and one for Queen Mary—with massive coachwork by Hooper. Nearly 5.5 metres (18 ft) in overall length, and claimed to be the largest private car in the world, the king's jubilee limousine had a wheelbase of about 4 metres (13 ft) compared with the longest Rolls-Royce Phantom II's equivalent figure of little more than 3.8 metres (12 ft 6 in)!

It is ironic, from a Lanchester viewpoint, that Daimler was not only to produce its own straight-eights for two decades, from 1934 to 1954, but also that several would be given Lanchester radiator grilles—notably those for the Duke of York (later King George VI) who liked Lanchester cars and wanted to support them.

The Lanchester name was to be dropped once and for all in 1956, and BSA had had enough of Daimler by 1960. The Daimler part of the business was sold to the successful and eager Jaguar company, desperate for factory space in Coventry. Jaguar does deserve passing mention in this chapter; but, whereas its later products could be rated among the world's best, the SS Jaguar was struggling for recognition, even in the late 1930s.

Like most car manufacturing nations, Britain once boasted a whole host of skilful coachbuilding companies. In the 1930s, however, some were finding it hard to make ends meet. As car makers fell by the wayside due to the slump, so did coachbuilders.

Hybrids and thoroughbreds

Nevertheless a number of body specialists were putting magnificent coachwork on mundane chassis. This was how Jaguar started, and it was an activity that led to the creation of other excellent but less successful makes. Some of these were of mixed nationality. Leading examples were the Hudson-based Brough Superior and Railton, and the Lammas-Graham. American cars had quite a strong following in those days despite the heavy horsepower tax, and Anglo-American hybrids, although lesser classics, had the added appeal of being both fashionable and comparatively cheap.

Tribute should, however, be paid to the way in which the Anglo-American Jensen car developed its own character. The Jensen brothers, Alan and Richard, had made an Austin Seven special when they were apprentices in the late 1920s. This was followed by a similar design on a Standard chassis—a model they sold to the Avon coachbuilding company of Warwick. After a brief period with the Patrick Motors Group, the Jensens formed their own company to make bodies for all sorts of vehicles, from racers to lorries. By the late 1930s, however, the straight-eight, Nash-powered Jensen car existed as a high quality saloon or convertible of great elegance. This elegance would be seen again after the war not only in its own cars but also in the Jensen bodywork for the prototype Meadows-engined Invicta Black Prince. The Invicta car had not been made since the mid-1930s, being replaced by the shortlived Hudson-powered Railton: the Black Prince was the Invicta's revival *and* its swansong. Jensen would continue to make several interesting cars under different managements for many years.

By contrast, the Lagonda, although American in name, was a thoroughly British car. Walter Owen Bentley had been pushed into a position of little or no influence by the 1931 Rolls-Royce takeover, but his skills as a great designer were not to be lost to British industry. Indeed, the creator of those majestic vintage sports cars went on to design one of the grandest of post-vintage tourers: the V12 Lagonda.

Towards the end of the 19th century Wilbur Gunn, an American, had brought the name Lagonda to Staines, Middlesex from Springfield, Ohio. (Lagonda was fur traders' French for the name given to a local river by the Shawnee Indians. They had called it 'Bucks' Horns' because it had so many creeks leading off it.) Early Lagondas built themselves a sporting image in the vintage years; this had reached a crescendo in the early 1930s with some excellent race results culminating in an unexpected Le Mans win in 1935 for the six-cylinder 4½-litre Meadows-engined M45R Rapide, a victory that coincided with the company's collapse.

For 1936, as chief designer, 'W.O.' gave the new Lagonda management hope for the future by pointing the marque in the direction of the luxury car market with his LG series. Then came the magnificent Bentley-designed V12 (also a 4½-litre), announced for 1937 but never pursued in the 1940s. It was the greatest of all Lagondas—and, perhaps, the best of the 'real Bentleys', too.

The 4.3-litre Alvis of the same period could also exceed 160 km/h (100 mph) and, clothed attractively by one or other of the top coachbuilders, such as Vanden Plas, looked just as beautiful, but did not have quite the same prestige. All the specialists were limited for finance, however, and Lea-Francis was a good example of the kind of company that spent most

of its time teetering on the brink of the collapse which came, inevitably, after World War II, despite the fact that the product itself was a good one.

There were many other great British cars of the 1930s, verging on the classic: there was the post-Nuffield MG SA saloon, hindered in its progress towards Grand Tourism only by the ascendancy of the SS Jaguar; there was the Talbot 105, best of the pre-Rootes group cars; there was the distinctive and underrated Rover whose four-light saloon still looked attractive when it was replaced by the famous 'Cyclops' type in 1949.

Big names like Austin and Humber went on producing large, well-crafted saloons and limousines in the 1930s. Although somewhat mundane it was a field in which the British shone: understated excellence without flamboyance.

American prestige cars

At the end of the 1930s, as war put an end to private car production, Rolls-Royce with Bentley, and Daimler (still under Royal patronage) remained the clear leaders among luxury British cars. North America, however, continued to turn out automobiles by the million. The war's early days hardly touched the great combines, whose classics were well established.

Chrysler survived its own special crisis in the 1930s caused largely by the eccentric Airflow, offered across the range as a Chrysler, a DeSoto, or an Imperial. The previous Imperial had been a splendid, well-balanced, all-American glamour car now regarded by many as a classic; the Airflow 'Custom Imperial' of 1936—arguably the originator of the one-piece curved windscreen—was a stylistic horror. In 1937, the Airflow's final production year, Chrysler returned to conventional styling for its top model, the Imperial C-15. The Airflow was copied almost immediately in Japan's Toyota AA and Sweden's Volvo PV36; both cars met with the same public disfavour as the

PRECEDING PAGES *A 1936 Rolls-Royce 25/30; Gurney Nutting sedanca de ville body.*

LEFT *The 1936 M.G. SA, intended to rival the SS.*

BELOW *Walter Owen Bentley competed against his former marque, which Rolls-Royce had acquired in 1931, when he designed this superb Lagonda LG45 of 1936.*

Airflow. Nevertheless, all three companies survived these classic blunders.

Ford had been making Lincoln its luxury line since 1922; and Lincoln's V12 engine was being produced in larger quantities than any other in the history of the automobile industry. The Zephyr and its more expensive Continental stablemate were beautifully styled, and the Lincoln became known as the Presidential marque from the days of Calvin Coolidge on.

General Motors used multi-cylinder engines and the Cadillac and Buick names to keep up its reputation. Each had its special slogan. Cadillac's claim was 'Standard of the World'; the other famous slogan was: 'When better Automobiles are built, Buick will build them'. Before his abdication, King Edward VIII managed to incur the silent diplomatic wrath of Daimler by buying a big black Buick; in fairness, it must have been Canadian and therefore at least from the British Commonwealth.

Coventry responded by making a Daimler straight-eight with American styling. The idea might have worked in the long run if Edward had remained on the throne. As it was, his brother succeeded him as George VI and stuck to the traditional Daimlers while retaining a liking for bespoke Lanchesters.

Most car manufacturing countries, as we have seen, still possessed skilled and traditional coachbuilding specialists, and the 1930s provided these with their last big opportunity for self-expression.

Wealthy Americans sometimes had special bodies built on European chassis; conversely, from time to time Europe's top coachbuilders would be presented with an American or Canadian chassis to clothe. Integral construction (chassis and body combined as one unit) would not be standard practice until the post-war era.

North American makers were well aware of the prestige attached to 'customizing', which always meant more if a coachbuilder's name was included—and there were some great artists in this field like Derham, Dietrich, Fisher, Judkins, LeBaron, Murphy, Rollston and Willoughby.

Outside the Big Three—the Chrysler, Ford and G.M. groups—Packard remained the leading and most influential practitioner among the big producers. This was partly due to the variety of coachwork available. Howard ('Dutch') Darrin, later of Kaiser-Frazer fame, created some of the most original and sporting bodies to be seen on Packards; and LeBaron's Sport Brougham design, also seen on Packards, was to be closely followed in Britain's good-looking post-war Morris Six and Wolseley 6/80. Packard's later partners, Studebaker, would not make styling history until after the war when Raymond Loewy introduced a lightness of touch that represented a milestone in motoring design. The other big names—Hudson and Nash, later to merge and form part of the nucleus of American Motors—were not producing true classics for the US customer in the 1930s, even if they were providing power units for some British companies mentioned previously.

The American independents

The Depression whittled away at the small independent car makers of America, and the early 1930s brought the demise of such great names as Franklin, Marmon and Stutz. However, two groups were still reaching the heights of bespoke engineering artistry. One of these was Pierce-Arrow. It is true that some of the later Pierce-Arrows had something of the Studebaker about their rounded lines, but they never lost their elegance altogether. It is probable that the marque would not have lasted as long as it did, had it not been helped by Studebaker finance, as mentioned earlier.

The Pierce-Arrow was always known for its built-in headlamps and aristocratic-looking radiator grille, and these were featured more strongly than ever in 1933 when the fabulous and eccentric Silver Arrow appeared at the World's Fair in Chicago. This was a serious streamlining attempt, with spare wheels hidden in enveloping wings; but it is believed that only five were made. By then, Studebaker had already disposed of the company to a group of enthusiastic financiers in the marque's home town of Buffalo, New York, who helped the magnificent Pierce-Arrow eights and twelves stay in production until 1938.

It is the Auburn-Cord-Duesenberg group, however, that stands out as the most fascinating of the classic American specialists. Auburn chief Errett Lobban Cord had bought Duesenberg in 1926, but did not put his own name to a car until three years later. Cord's marketing skill and imagination helped his three marques through the early years of the Depression. In 1932, the first and only 12-cylinder car ever to be offered at under $1000 was the 6.4-litre Auburn. Cord used the skill of Gordon Buehrig to help Auburn; but Buehrig's real claim to fame is in the styling of the second generation of Cord cars. These amazing-looking saloons and convertibles had sleek low bodies without running boards, and the headlamps were hidden in the mudguards. (There was a handle to wind the lamps out for use.) Bonnet and grille were plain and severe by the usual American standards, and the originality of the Cord body was such that it was granted a patent in May 1934.

Besides its looks, the 1935 Cord 810 had the front-wheel drive of its predecessor, the L-29, and mechanical individuality was enhanced by the added features of independent front suspension, plus a vacuum gearchange that allowed electric preselection (see page 57) from a small steering column gate.

Sadly, the new Cords were not delivered on time because of serious transmission problems. The ultimate Cord—the 1937 long-wheelbase Type 812 with supercharged V8 Lycoming engine—could exceed 160 km/h (100 mph) with ease, but also priced itself out of the market.

During a short life, from 1935 to 1937, fewer than 2500 examples of America's futuristic Cord 810/812 were manufactured, and those that survived are now prized treasures. Such was the admiration for these models that there were several attempts in the post-war years to re-create the Cord and market it.

Back in the 1930s, the shape lived on, to keep two other industrial casualties going for a while. Norman deVaux, who had tried unsuccessfully to make cars of his own on two occasions, was on hand when the Cord body dies were being sold for scrap. He bought them and, as a result, the distinctive Cord shape was still current in 1941, four years after Cord's collapse.

What deVaux did was to exchange these dies for $50,000 and a place on the board of the Hupp Corporation, which was foundering because its Hupmobile Aerodynamic (although much better looking than Chrysler's Airflow) had been too modern for public taste, and the rest of the range too dull.

Hupp needed a new car urgently, and the Hupmobile Skylark was created virtually overnight. What no one had calculated was the cost of assembling the Buehrig body, for in the Cord days it had been a labour-intensive activity, in line with the high cost of the car. After 30 or 40 Skylarks had been made deVaux, realizing Hupp could not put the bodies together economically, went to see another failing Detroit

LEFT *Skilful use by Cadillac of GM's technical and marketing facilities kept the marque ahead in the American glamour car business: 1931 Model 370 roadster with rumble rear seat.*

BELOW *Lincoln Continental of 1942 shows style, but gives warning of the excessive chrome and 'heaviness' that was to mar the looks of most post-war American cars.*

company, Graham-Paige. Here he arranged that Graham would undertake the required bodymaking, welding, and metal finishing for Hupp; and in return Graham-Paige, too, could have a new car of its own—the Hollywood! Graham's existing pointed-nose styling was almost as unusual as Hupp's Aerodynamic saloon. Certainly custom was being lost daily. Both firms jumped at the idea of selling cars that looked like Cords, but without the troublesome pop-up headlamps. The production figures for these virtually identical-looking cars are thought to be around 350 Hupmobile Skylarks and 2000 Graham Hollywoods in the 1939–41 period.

Despite the small quantities, these strange alliances did enable both companies to take on war contracts and live a little longer than they might otherwise have done. Owning one of these cars (which had rear-wheel drive) would be a good way of enjoying Buehrig's exciting design without the worry and distress of having to contend with the under-developed Cord transmission. (Individual enthusiasts need not necessarily be deterred by the fact that classic car clubs might not regard the Graham and the Hupmobile marques as worthy of their interest!)

This chapter cannot be concluded without reference to the third victim of the fall of the Cord empire in 1937. The Duesenberg may not have been as sophisticated or as meticulously finished as a Rolls-Royce or Hispano-Suiza, but of all America's early classics it was the mightiest. It did not join Cadillac and Marmon in making 16-cylinder engines. Instead it offered a 7-litre straight-eight, with double overhead camshafts, giving out over 300 bhp in SJ (supercharged) form. Road performance was, therefore, little affected by the Duesenberg's enormous size and weight.

Fred Duesenberg was killed as a result of a crash in 1932, but his brother August continued to work for E.L. Cord on Auburn and Duesenberg projects, and even tried to revive his own marque in the 1940s. Auburn, Cord and Duesenberg were all to be revived in various forms by post-war enthusiasts because each had had a very special appeal in its day. Truly, E.L. Cord's trio represented the ultimate in North American classicism. The next era would see automation, power-assistance, more speed limits, more road regulations. America has pioneered many things, among them the inevitable, unending process of limiting man's use of the very machine that had brought him his freedom of the road in the first place.

RIGHT *Off-white elephant: the Pierce-Arrow was remarkable in all its forms. It had built-in headlamps from 1913, and impressive looks right to its lingering end in 1938, despite some concessions to pressed-steel bodymaking techniques—as seen in this 1936 Type 1602 V12 Club Sedan.*

BELOW *By the mid-1930s the Pierce-Arrow had begun to lose its way, but Cord design was bringing a breath of fresh air in its startlingly original patented Buehrig styling. Some models (not this 1936 Type 810 Westchester Sedan) had exposed exhaust pipes, and all had retractable headlamps.*

SPORTS CARS OF THE 1930s

No book on the early classics would be complete without a section on sports cars. There is no simple and comprehensive definition of a sports car, except that it generally has above average responsiveness and performance. Historically, sports cars have been much involved in competition and few true sporting marques have not won laurels in races or rallies, or both.

France has always been regarded as the home of international motor racing, and the 24-hour race of Le Mans is the world's most famous motoring contest. Perhaps less dominant in its field than it used to be, the Monte Carlo Rally, which takes place mostly in France, is also a very important event to win.

In the vintage years the 24-hour Grand Prix d'Endurance at Le Mans had been the domain of Britain's big Bentleys, which won five of the first eight races. Then Alfa Romeo of Italy took victory four times (1931 to 1934); but in 1937, when a French car won for the first time in 11 years, it was thanks to the revered name of Bugatti.

Until the German invasion of the Grand Prix scene in 1934, Bugatti was still a leading light there; after that, the only chance of France remaining prominent in competition would lie in sports car racing. In 1936, the French GP was, conveniently, made a sports car event, and Bugatti produced a streamlined version of the Type 57—the last of Molsheim's road-car designs. It won the 1000 km race and went on to give France victory at Le Mans in 1937 and 1939. Those supercharged racing-sports cars performed very impressively, but their tank-like appearance was not typically Bugatti. On the other hand it would be difficult to imagine a more scintillating combination of mechanical and visual delight than was to be found in the roadgoing Type 57s, with their graceful fixed-head coupé bodywork designed by Jean Bugatti. Technically obsolescent they may have been; but they can, with reason, be called the original Grand Touring cars.

Several updated Type 57s were to appear after World War II as the Type 101, but the inspiration had gone: first with the accident to Jean in 1939 (see previous chapter), and then the death in 1947 of Ettore himself. Although there would be final, dramatic, abortive attempts to go GP racing again as late as 1956, the Bugatti's day was done.

The only other French marque to win Le Mans in the 1930s was Delahaye; the year was 1938, and the race was one of attrition with the fastest cars retiring. A Delahaye would have won that year's Monte Carlo Rally too, but for a simple mistake in the final test; however, the marque did win the event in 1937 and 1939. (Here, Hotchkiss should be mentioned again, as one of the most successful of all Monte Carlo Rally marques, although the company could hardly qualify as a sports car manufacturer as it almost invariably produced

touring cars in the period in question.)

Delage, once the maker of great racing cars, was still in business, although from 1935 the company came under Delahaye's control. Delage did well several times at Le Mans without ever winning; but in 1938 the marque showed its continuing excellence by taking the British Tourist Trophy back to France for a second successive year. The TT, first held in 1905, is Britain's longest-established motor race. In the late 1930s it was run on the Donington Park circuit near Loughborough in Leicestershire; the 1937 winner was a French Talbot, referred to in Britain as a Darracq to avoid confusion with the British Talbot. This complication had arisen when the Sunbeam-Talbot-Darracq company collapsed and the French factory came under the control of Antonio Lago. The French marque was later identified more clearly when it became known as Talbot-Lago.

Although these great machines were—apart from Alfa Romeo—probably the world's fastest practical roadgoing sports cars of the 1930s, it must be remembered that France produced many small sports cars, too. In fact, the French had been leaders in this field before the arrival of the British, led by M.G.

The big three French companies, Citroën, Peugeot, and Renault, tended to concentrate on long-distance records during this decade. Their most realistic compromise between performance and price was the streamlined 2-litre Peugeot Type 402, as modified by Emile Darl'Mat, which proved itself an instant classic of reliability by coming 7th, 8th and 10th at Le Mans in 1937, and taking 5th place in 1938. (This rare model is illustrated on page 39.)

The earliest of the classic French producers, Panhard, did not make sports cars in the immediate post-war period. The company was in desperate need of a new theme, and World War II provided the breathing space to find one—the result was a totally new concept.

J.A. Grégoire, a leading exponent of front-wheel drive since introducing the Tracta marque in 1926, spent much of the German Occupation period developing cars for the future. As early as 1942, with the cooperation of the Aluminium Français company, Grégoire had built a small, independently sprung, lightweight prototype, powered by a twin-cylinder air-cooled engine. By the time of the liberation of France in 1944 the car was ready for production. Plans to make it in Australia, Britain and the United States all came to naught, but in France the design gave Panhard a new lease of life. The little Dyna-Panhard, as it was called, had a fine performance and formed the basis for a variety of post-war French competition cars. (Panhard would eventually be absorbed by Citroën, which was already ruled financially by the mighty Michelin tyre company.)

PRECEDING PAGES *1939 SS Jaguar 100, Britain's first 100 mph car at under £500.*

LEFT *Beautiful sports and GT bodies were built on the Bugatti Type 57 chassis: a 1938 example by Guillore.*

BELOW *Probably a 'Darracq' to Britons at the time, this attractive 1938 Talbot-Lago is closely related to the successful competition models. These did even better after the war when they won several Grands Prix and the 24-hour race at Le Mans.*

The Italian contribution

It is much easier to pinpoint the outstanding sports cars of Italy, a nation that expresses its love of motoring dramatically through the feats of its great engineers, stylists and drivers. Alfa Romeo and Maserati were the great sporting marques.

Most Maseratis were pure racers; the company made few true sports cars (as opposed to single-seaters) until after World War II. Thus the Maserati name never appeared on the roll of honour of that classic Italian road race, the Mille Miglia.

With one exception every Mille Miglia of the 1930s was won by Alfa Romeo. In fact the marque came second every time as well! These successes at home, with innumerable victories elsewhere, including those four at Le Mans, placed Nicola Romeo's machines firmly at the top of the sports car league. Most credit for this must go to Tazio Nuvolari and Vittorio Jano.

Nuvolari was the greatest of all Italian racing drivers, and the only man ever to defeat the might of a full field of Auto Union and Mercedes-Benz competitors; this he did with a special Alfa Romeo P3 single-seater in the 1935 German Grand Prix.

Jano was Alfa Romeo's chief designer. He had come from FIAT in the mid-1920s and soon gave his new employers a fine double overhead camshaft six-cylinder engine. This was

BELOW *One of Vittorio Jano's masterpieces: the Alfa Romeo 8C 2300, a model that had many race victories, including four in a row at Le Mans, from 1931 to 1934. This 1932 car was bodied by Touring.*

RIGHT *The FIAT Balilla of 1935 was Italy's bargain sports car and formed the basis for a number of specials. It was an adaptation of an 1100 cc light car, yet dominated its class in racing. As neat and nimble in its day as the little X1/9 is now.*

followed in 1931 by a beautiful straight-eight, which began life at 2.3 litres but was enlarged for both road and race cars.

Undaunted—apparently—by the economic depression, which led to the nationalization of the company in 1933, Alfa Romeo continued to take advantage of Jano's great designs, and between 1937 and 1939 offered a limited number of independently sprung 8C 2900B sports cars. In 1937, when transmission trouble caused the retirement of a new V12 racing car from the 1937 Italian Grand Prix, quite unfairly poor Jano was dismissed. As a result, the designer of one of the greatest sports cars the world has seen took his talent to Lancia. Jano's post-war Aurelia was to be one of the most important modern classic GT cars; Alfa's loss was Lancia's gain.

By the 1930s, FIAT was not racing in the big league; but the company won many of the smaller car classes with the neat little Tipo 508 FIAT Balilla. This was the model that led France to produce FIATs under licence as Simcas, and Amédée Gordini to build his own even sportier versions of the marque. It also gave rise to a number of special Italian sports cars—including one unforgettable classic.

Back in 1920 a young man from Modena had joined Alfa Romeo as a team driver, and in the years that followed he also proved himself to be a first-class combination of administrator and organizer. One of his actions, for example, was to persuade Alfa Romeo and Jano that they should work together.

At the end of 1929, the young man left to set up in Modena, taking with him the blessing of Alfa Romeo—in the form of its motor racing organization. From then until 1938 the official Alfa Romeo racing team was called the Scuderia Ferrari. Now not so young, Enzo Ferrari soon gave up racing himself, for he was never in the top class, but he made sure that some of the world's finest drivers drove for his team.

Then, in 1938, Alfa Corse was created by Alfa Romeo; it was to be a works-run racing team, based in Milan. Ferrari tried to make the change, but found working for someone else again unsatisfactory, despite his closeness to the Alfa Romeo company for so many years. He returned to his garage in Modena to set up on his own as Auto Avio Costruzioni.

Ferrari's decision to make his own cars came soon afterwards when he received two approaches for machines to be raced in the Mille Miglia. The plans were laid by Christmas 1939, and the two cars were completed in time for the race on 28 April 1940. Chief designer of these first 'Ferrari' cars was Alberto Massimino, and the basis was the ubiquitous FIAT 508—not only for chassis components but also in the use of two cylinder heads fitted over a special straight-eight cylinder block. Bodied by Touring, the two streamlined cars led their class in turn, only to retire with mechanical trouble. Part of Enzo Ferrari's severance agreement with Alfa Romeo had been not to use his name on a car for a set period, because it was associated so closely with Alfa Romeo's. Those first two 'Ferraris', made by AAC of Modena, are therefore known historically by their type number: 815 (eight cylinders, 1.5 litres).

The first cars actually to bear the name Ferrari were undoubtedly conceived during the war, but the V12 Ferrari was not described in print until 1946, and therefore the rest of the Ferrari story belongs to the modern classic period. Ferrari cars began winning races in 1947 and the success has never ceased.

German sports cars

Only one other country was producing truly classic sports cars in continental Europe during this period and that, of course, was Germany. The Avusrennen, held on a purpose-built road near Berlin, had been won in 1931 and 1932 by Mercedes-Benz. In 1933, however, the year the Nazis came to power, this important home event was a walkover for Bugatti of

France and Alfa Romeo of Italy. Anxious to restore German prestige, the government put sufficient money into the newly formed Auto Union and the well-established Daimler-Benz companies to ensure the virtual eclipse of all the opposition in Grand Prix racing from 1934, and also cleverly created a genuine competition between the two German teams.

Neither company took part in international sports car events in this period, however, but in the early part of the decade the massive Mercedes-Benz SSK and SSKL had had some spectacular results. The marque would have won Le Mans in 1931 but for tyre trouble; and the German star, Rudolf Caracciola—arguably the greatest racing driver of the decade—beat the Italians by brute force and brilliance when he won that year's Mille Miglia.

At home, German marques spent much of the time taking part in military-style cross-country trials. The few monster sports cars still made in the Hitler period were for his top men and would not have been agile enough for rally-type events. Mercedes-Benz did find time to make the 150H, a rear-engined sports car developed from its unsuccessful 130H saloon, but it was a complete failure too.

Only two German sports cars really impressed the outside world in these years. Adler made an excellent showing in the Alpine Trials and the long-distance sports car races. Its streamlined 1.7-litre *Rennlimousine* did well to come 6th at Le Mans two years running in 1937 and 1938.

However, by far the most significant German sports car to emerge was the BMW, for which Sir Herbert Austin is to be thanked! It will be recalled how, in the late vintage era, Austin Sevens were being made under licence by Dixi, shortly before that company's acquisition by BMW (see chapter two). Fritz Fiedler—formerly of Stoewer and Horch—was the designer who, using the Austin only as a base, moved BMW very quickly out of the ordinary and ahead of its rivals. His small Sixes of 1.5 and 2 litres were nimble and attractive, and the Type 328 can be regarded as the true epitome of a sports car, for it was reasonably priced, yet could outshine most of the opposition on the race track, in rallies, or in trials of the kind in which road grip was of prime importance. Popular in Britain for these reasons, the BMW scored excellent results in such widely differing events as the Land's End or Exeter Trials, the Tourist Trophy race and the RAC Rally. Streamlined versions demolished the Alfa Romeo opposition in the 1940 Mille Miglia.

BELOW *Caracciola (Mercedes-Benz, No 7) beat Rosemeyer (rear-engined Auto Union) in the 1935 Eifelrennen. Chiron (Alfa Romeo) was third. His skill, and team mate Nuvolari's, kept the Italian GP cars in touch with the Germans at the start of this era of racing.*

RIGHT AND INSET *The very modern BMW 328 of 1936.*

M-HU 4804

BTF 72

PRECEDING PAGES *The 1936 M.G. TA Midget.*

ABOVE *The 1932-4 Aston Martin Series II Le Mans $1\frac{1}{2}$-litre model designed by Bertelli.*

RIGHT *Before the Nuffield take-over Riley produced a variety of sports cars of great—and fully exploited—competition potential. This is a 1936 model Sprite.*

The outstanding driver A.F. Agabeg (who changed his name to A.F.P. Fane) had won his class for BMW in 1938 when the great round-Italy road race had featured one fatal accident too many, and the Italian authorities cried 'enough' for 1939. The 1940 revival, six months after the outbreak of World War II, was given a different format. It was held over nine laps of a fast triangular road circuit, based (as usual) on Brescia and described as the 'Brescia Grand Prix'. This strange event was a BMW versus Alfa Romeo battle—resolved with the Italian-styled BMWs sandwiching the best Alfa. The winning BMW prototype developed an estimated 130 bhp from under 2 litres, yet averaged well over 160 km/h (100 mph).

British variety

More than anywhere else, Britain made itself the true home of the sports car. Perhaps it was lightheartedness or simple love of sport; and certainly there was no lack of the competitive spirit. There is no doubt that the British sports car of the 1930s paved the way for the export successes that were to come after the war.

Britain's biggest producer of the decade was the Nuffield Organization. Morris cars already had a good name for reliability when the local dealership in Oxford—Morris Garages, run by Cecil Kimber—had begun modifying them in the 1920s. Thus was born the M.G. which was able to give the driver of modest means pleasure and enjoyment, yet also won the Tourist Trophy race no fewer than three times: 1931, 1933 (driven by the great Nuvolari) and 1934. M.G. motoring for two decades from the mid-1930s was typified by the delightful T series Midgets—which saw the wooing of so many wartime brides.

Mention of the TT leads naturally to Bentley. With Rolls-Royce in control of its destiny, the Bentley's racing heritage lay in those five vintage victories at Le Mans; yet the 'Rolls-Bentley' did have a racing career—thanks to Eddie Hall, who came second on handicap in the last three Ulster TT races of 1934, 1935 and 1936. Because he did not quite win, Hall's incredible performances with what was, basically, a Rolls-Royce 20/25 will never receive the recognition they deserve—nor will his final fling with the car after the war, which brought him eighth place at Le Mans in 1950!

Perhaps it is fairest to take the rest of the British sports car classics alphabetically, for no other nation made such a variety of them. John Weller's 2-litre engine, first seen in 1919, stayed in production with the London company, AC, for over 40 years. A light alloy overhead camshaft unit, it had powered Britain's first Monte Carlo Rally winner in 1926. Then, in 1933, Kitty Brunell (daughter of the most prolific of the early motoring photographers) put up best performance in the RAC Rally, and the AC's reputation for watch-like precision as Britain's original Light Six was secure.

The Allard by contrast was far from precise, being a big Ford V8- or Lincoln V12-powered trials special with divided front axle. Its classic feature was its development by Sydney Allard into a car capable of winning the Monte Carlo and RAC Rallies, *and* coming third at Le Mans, in the early post-war years.

The accomplished driver Peter Whitehead cut his teeth with a twin-camshaft 1100 cc Alta which he raced and sprinted and drove in trials. The Alta went on to become a Grand Prix car. Alvis had had similar hopes with its front-wheel drive cars but these were not successful; the sporting post-vintage Alvis machines were more orthodox, and the 12/50 and 12/70 models gained numerous race victories.

Aston Martin survived several management changes to prove itself a worthy class winner in such widely differing events as the Mille Miglia, Le Mans and the Alpine Trial. (This pedigree was to lead, ultimately, to victory in the 1959 World Sports Car Championship.)

Supercharging and overhead camshafts gave Murray Jamieson's modified Austin Sevens a performance quite remarkable for their minute size but, as we have seen, the Austin's real role was as Britain's 'Motor for the Millions'. The Frazer Nash, on the other hand, was eccentric in that it harked back to the vintage G.N. (Godfrey and Nash) cyclecar. Even in the mid-1930s, despite its powerful engine, the Frazer Nash remained old fashioned with its chain-drive transmission. Foreseeing the problems of trying to make a living solely from such a car, company boss H.J. Aldington began looking for an alternative product and found it while competing in the 1934 Alpine Trial. The new BMW sports car clearly handled and held the road so much better, and he soon persuaded the German company to let him look after its UK sales. The traditional Frazer Nash remained in limited production while the name Frazer Nash-BMW was coined to make the German car seem British. The cars were later to benefit from the release from detention of BMW's Fritz Fiedler to create a post-war Frazer Nash. At the end of the war the main BMW car factory ended up in the Soviet zone of newly divided Germany. BMW would not start producing cars in Munich until 1952.

Although no British sports cars of the day matched the six-cylinder, 2-litre BMW with its rigid chassis and modern handling, there was certainly no shortage of choice for the enthusiast—and there were several proprietary makes of engine, too, such as the 1½-litre, four-cylinder Meadows used by E. A. Halford, G. H. Robins and H. R. Godfrey for their traditional-style lightweight two-seater, launched from a Surrey workshop in 1936. Their HRG proved itself straight away by good placings at Le Mans and in the RAC Rally, and wartime saw a streamlined version under development.

Another Meadows user was the Invicta; but this was a very different car. The 4½-litre, six-cylinder engine, designed for military use, gave the car excellent top-gear flexibility. Moreover, the long, low lines and the imposing riveted bonnet made the sports model look just the high-performer it was. Donald Healey, later an untiring car maker of considerable distinction, used an Invicta to win the Monte Carlo Rally of 1931—by no means an isolated demonstration of the car's capabilities. Some of the aura was carried on in the lower-priced Hudson-based Railton which replaced the Invicta in the middle of the decade.

Lagonda, too, used the 'big six' Meadows engine to put up good race performances in the 1934–6 period, including that remarkable Le Mans win. W.O. Bentley's V12-powered Lagondas of 1937, usually built as luxury touring cars, also saw competition service as tuned two-seaters. Their third and fourth places at Le Mans in 1939 reflect strict team discipline rather than any inability of the marque to win outright for a second time. How David Brown brought Lagonda and Aston Martin together is a post-war story.

Lea-Francis and Morgan make an interesting contrast. After its high point—a 1928 TT win—Lea-Francis staggered from crisis to crisis, with good cars but insufficient inspiration for the limited yet crowded sports car market. Morgan, however, stayed small, moving with the times when necessary—notably by changing from three wheels to four. Morgan is unique in

having stayed in business, and today every car that leaves the small family-run factory among the lovely Malvern Hills is a reminder of what Britain has lost since the days of the early classics.

The M.G. name, too, is still alive in a marketing sense, but it is too late now for a Riley resurrection; yet, like M.G., Rileys won the TT race three times, in 1932, 1935 and 1936, and in 1934 one came second at Le Mans! A measure of the soundness of the Riley's concept was that Freddie Dixon and Raymond Mays adapted it for speed work. Indeed Mays's 'White Riley' sprint car led to the ERA, Britain's most famous and effective pre-war single-seater racer. With Riley and M.G., the little Singer was probably the most familiar two-seater on Britain's sporting scene – and it had been the marque that inspired the first Aston Martin.

Perfectionists and survivors

Manufacturers who fail to get their cars into production hardly qualify for classic status. There have been many men in Britain and elsewhere whose cars have been doomed as production types by their very brilliance and originality; and there is a classic case of this.

'No attempt has been missed to make the Squire car the owner-driver's ideal.' Thus ended the text of a six-page catalogue of 1925, written and illustrated by a 16-year-old schoolboy called Adrian Squire, who went on to work for Bentley and M.G. From 1931, however, he began to realize his dream and in 1934 the first Squire car was running. The supercharged twin-camshaft engine developed over 100 bhp, but was of only 1½-litre capacity. A lowest price of £1200 may have been inevitable because of the built-in perfectionism, but a Bugatti could be bought for that, and the small size of Squire's special Anzani engine probably did much to put off potential customers. Ten Squire cars were built, three of them from parts after the company was wound up in 1936. Adrian Squire went to work for W.O. Bentley again at Lagonda. He was killed in an air raid on the Bristol Aircraft factory where he was employed during World War II. Most of the cars survive; especially beautiful is the Vanden Plas-bodied two-seater in the world's biggest car collection created by the late William Harrah in Reno, Nevada.

Walter Hassan was a survivor of that same Bristol air attack in which Squire died. He was soon to return to Coventry and play a key part in the creation of the XK engine and Jaguar's post-war programme. Like Squire, Hassan had begun his engineering training with Bentley, and his work at Brooklands race track was already legendary. In the late 1930s he had been development engineer under William Heynes at SS Cars, the company that became Jaguar. The sharply sculptured sporting lines of the 1936 SS Jaguar 100 two-seater bore some similarity to those of the Squire—but this resemblance was only skin-deep.

Swallow Coachbuilding had been renamed SS; but the cars themselves were, until 1935, based on other people's engineering. Bill Heynes's arrival as chief engineer marked the birth of the new marque SS Jaguar. In 1937 the six-cylinder, 2.7-litre overhead valve engine was supplemented by a 3½-litre version, and overnight SS was offering Britain's first under-£500 car capable of a genuine 160 km/h (100 mph). At £445 for the attractive, compact, big-engined Jaguar 100, SS chief William Lyons's salesmanship undercut the £695 of an important new rally rival, the Frazer Nash-BMW 328, and left no room at all for the Adrian Squires of this world—even if the product itself might not bear such close technical scrutiny. Heynes and Hassan developed the SS Jaguars with diligence, however, and the marque's reputation soared while Lyons kept strict control of the business reins—as he would do until his retirement in 1972. Among the firms Lyons watched going rapidly downhill as war approached was his nearest neighbour in Coventry, Triumph, despite Donald Healey's energetic

work on the Dolomite. Lyons simply tightened his belt another notch—one reason why the Jaguar lives.

At the height of this period of rapid growth, William Lyons attempted to buy the assets of Sunbeam—a great name in vintage racing, but a shadow of its former self. However, William Rootes beat him to it in a move that also brought about the destruction of the Georges Roesch-designed British Talbot. The team of Talbot 105s that raced and rallied so effectively 50 years ago is remarkable in that it has survived—the cars are all in the collection of Talbot's champion and historian, Anthony Blight.

In the United States motoring competitions for European-type sports cars hardly existed in the 1930s. They were confined to the races held in the grounds of the home of the wealthy Collier family near New York, and a few subsequent events culminating in a race around the New York World's Fair ground in 1940.

The fabulous Auburn, Duesenberg and Stutz all lived on into the 1930s, but they had been created in vintage times. The most advanced competition cars to come from the USA were, in fact, the pure racers of the genius Harry Miller, which were unbeatable on so many occasions in the Indianapolis 500-mile race.

Ettore Bugatti's admiration for Miller's work undoubtedly influenced the most distinguished sports cars in the world, so nothing could be more appropriate than to end this chapter on sports cars in the way it began by acknowledging the greatest and most beautiful of them all: Bugatti, the ultimate classic.

RIGHT *Last of the great American sports cars, the Duesenberg died with the Cord group in 1937, shortly after this SSJ was made. There have been at least four attempted revivals*

LEFT *Morgan is notable for surviving so long as a family-run firm. From 1910 to 1950 it led the world in three-wheelers like this 1933 V-twin JAP-powered Super Sports.*

BELOW *Varzi (Bugatti Type 51, No 10) and Nuvolari (Alfa Romeo Monza, No 26) contesting the 1933 Monaco GP. These two marques battled for supremacy in the early 1930s.*

INDEX

Page numbers in *italics* refer to captions to illustrations

Acknowledgements

The publishers wish to thank the following organizations and individuals for their kind permission to reproduce the photographs in this book:
Auburn-Cord-Duesenberg Museum 64–5; Neill Bruce Endpapers, 1, 4–5, 12, 13 below, 20 inset, 22–3, 24–5, 26–7, 30, 33, 50–1, 56–7, 70, 76, 77, 78; *Classic and Sportscar* (Mel Drew) 43, 51; Conservatoire National des Arts et Métiers 8, 9; Ian Dawson/Octopus Books 34, 45 above, 60–1, 66–7, 79 above; Geoffrey Goddard 20–1, 48–9; Jaguar-Daimler Photographic Department 32–3; Chris Linton/Octopus Books 2–3, 6–7, 30–1, 58–9, 74–5; Long Island Automotive Museum, N.Y./Henry Austin Clark Jr 19 above, 35, 46–7, 62, 63; Andrew Morland 36–7; National Motor Museum, Beaulieu 17, 18, 70–1; Charles Pocklington 26 left; Cyril Posthumus 29 above, 41 inset, 52 inset, 79 below; Renault, France 13 above; Peter Roberts 15, 16, 19 below, 26 right, 38–9, 42, 44, 72 left; Bobbie'dine Rodda 65; Rainer Schlegelmilch/Octopus Books 10, 11, 28–9, 54 inset, 72–3; Halwart Schrader 39, 40–1, (Wieslaw Fusaro) 54–5; Andrew J. Whyte 45 below; Nicky Wright/Octopus Books 14–15; Franco Zagari 25, 29 above, 52–3, 61, 68–9

In addition, the publishers wish to thank the following:
The Bicton Hall of Transport, BMW Museum, Briggs Cunningham Automotive Museum, D. Buller-Sinfield, Roger Cook, Leyland Heritage, Long Island Automotive Museum, N.Y., Richard Lowe, Tom Mason, Mercedes-Benz Museum, Midland Motor Museum, Kenneth Neve, Nigel Dawes Collection, Rex Sevier, Keith Storey, Michael Turvill.

PDO 83-585

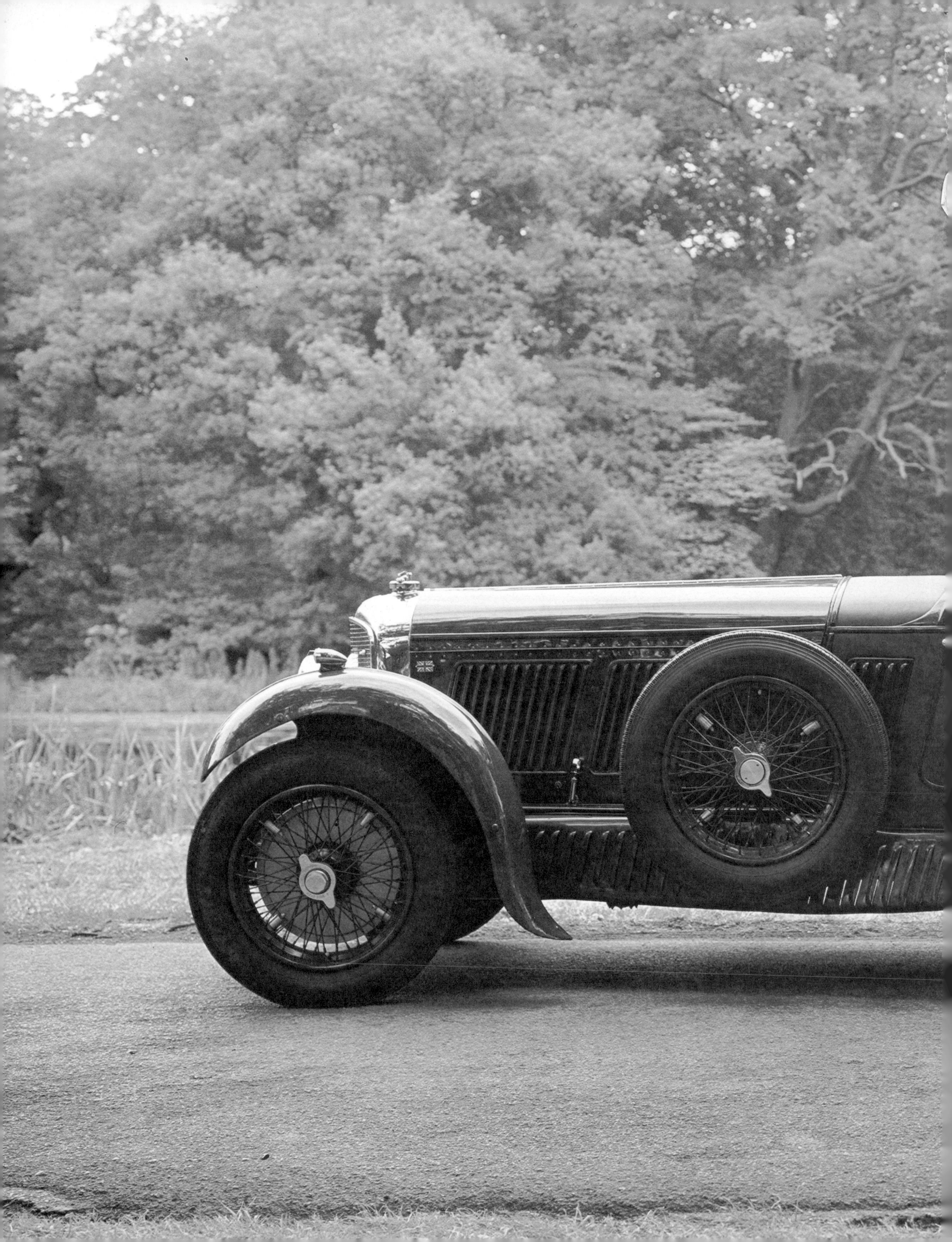